2002

The Third Shift
Women Learning Online

By Cheris Kramarae
1999-2000 AAUW Educational Foundation Scholar-in-Residence

Special thanks to the members of AAUW of Virginia
for making this project possible through their visionary leadership
and generous financial support.

Published by the American Association of University Women Educational Foundation
1111 Sixteenth St. N.W.
Washington, DC 20036
Phone: 202/728-7602
Fax: 202/463-7169
TDD: 202/785-7777
foundation@aauw.org
www.aauw.org

First printing: August 2001
Editor: Susan K. Dyer
Layout and design: Julie A. Hamilton
Cover design: Sabrina Meyers

Library of Congress Card Number: 2001093546
ISBN: 1-879922-29-0

029-02 8/01 7.0M

Table of Contents

Acknowledgments

I am thankful to the American Association of University Women Educational Foundation for the initiation and support of this study of gender and online higher education. AAUW has a long and respected history of leadership in investigating issues of gender and education and publishing studies and reports that are action catalysts for educators, administrators, students, and policy-makers.

Higher education in the United States is undergoing dramatic changes. University students in most courses now use the web either to fulfill course requirements or to supplement assignments. Furthermore, the growth in courses developed entirely for online delivery has risen sharply in the last few years. This report highlights problems, possibilities, and concerns raised by hundreds of the women and men who are participating in the vast changes in continuing education.

I thank AAUW Educational Foundation Director of Research Pamela Haag for her many useful suggestions and her skillful help with the structure of the report and Sue Dyer for her editing and suggestions for clarification. I also acknowledge the women and men of AAUW of Virginia for their support of this project during the organization's celebration of 75 years of membership and activism.

Thank you also to the students and faculty at the 2000 International Women's University in Germany (Internationale Frauenuniversität [www.ifu.de]), especially those in the Reconstruction of Gender on the Internet and in the Future of Education projects for providing valuable perspectives regarding these issues. Pamela Saunders provided initial suggestions for the structure of this study.

I appreciate the work of three AAUW interns who provided assistance with this project. Timothy Mitchell, a second-year graduate student in the Communication, Culture, and Technology Program at Georgetown University in Washington, D.C., conducted many face-to-face and telephone interviews with people in a wide variety of occupations. Veronique Dozier, program coordinator for the African Studies Program at Georgetown University, also conducted interviews. Alexa Champion, a graduate student focusing on media studies in the Communication, Culture, and Technology Program at Georgetown University, assisted with the search for literature about online higher education.

Special thanks go to the hundreds of participants who, via questionnaires, interviews, and discussion groups, shared their experiences and their ideas about online education.

—Cheris Kramarae

Part 1

Introduction

 Universities in the United States are undergoing dramatic changes as they respond to a competitive global economy, stunning new technological opportunities, and the increased need for and interest in continuing education courses and programs. At the same time, higher education has become more market-oriented and, according to some critics, more hostile to the development of inclusive education in universities. Computer technology has been at the heart of many of the changes, and it has transformed the delivery of education, the development and dissemination of knowledge, and communications between students and scholars. While some administrators and educators predict that bits and bytes will replace brick and mortar in the high-tech college of the 21st century, others are dubious that technology has or will change the fundamentals of education and university learning—for better or worse.

The Third Shift

In 1989 sociologist Arlie Russell Hochschild published a landmark study of work and family conflicts in which she introduced the metaphor of a "second shift" for women in the home. Most women, she explains, "work one shift at the office or factory and a 'second shift' at home," culminating in the equivalent of an extra month of work over the course of a year. One interviewee explained that although she resisted the idea that homemaking was a "shift," she did feel that "you're on duty at work. You come home, and you're on duty. Then you go back to work and you're on duty." As Hochschild concludes, "Her home life *felt* like a second shift."

This report elaborates Hochschild's still-timely metaphor of work and family life. It adds education to the equation as a third shift—in addition to paid work and work in the home—for many female students. As lifelong learning and knowledge become ever more important to economic well-being, women and men find they juggle not only work and family, but also demands of further schooling and education throughout their lives. In this report, women students describe how they grapple individually, often in isolation, with time constraints so they can unobtrusively squeeze distance learning into their already packed work and family lives. Through distance education, technology offers new opportunities for many women to achieve educational goals. This report explores why women pursue the third shift; how they manage to balance work, family, and education; and what would make distance learning easier for them.

Coming to Terms: What Is Distance Education?

The terms "online education" and "distance learning" refer to a system and process of connecting students, teachers, and learning resources when they are not in the same location. (Distance education has been tied to communication technologies for many years in the United States, initially after the establishment of an efficient postal system.) In the past several decades, the format of distance education has changed from primarily paper-based instruction to integrated multimedia (such as the delivery of courses via TV programs) to the use of networked computers (the Internet) and the World Wide Web—a part of the Internet that consists of "pages" (documents, which can include pictures and sounds) linked to each other. Internet-based distance education is becoming the major delivery method in the United States and often is referred to as online education, distance learning, web-based learning, computer-based training, distributed learning, or e-learning. Australia and some European countries also use the terms "flexible learning," "managed learning," and "open learning."

What was once a division between online education and e-learning is becoming blurred as universities form partnerships with businesses and each other to better compete in a greatly expanded global market for students. Some people in business talk about continuing or adult education primarily in terms of modules that can be taken when new skills are needed for particular tasks. Most study respondents believe, however, that providing skill training, while necessary for many people and businesses, is not the same as helping prepare students for long-term effective functioning in a variety of situations in a diverse society.

The growth of distance education resulted from many factors, including the following:

- Decreases in government subsidies of the public institutions of higher education

- Increases in costs of higher education at both public and private institutions

- Increases in the number of employed women

- Reductions in secure, long-term jobs

- Increases in credential requirements for entry to and continuing work in many jobs

- Rapid changes in information technologies

- Increases in online business

- Increases in venture capital funding in knowledge enterprises

- Increases in college enrollments

- Increases in attention to lifelong education

- Increases in competition among institutions for education dollars

- Increases in the globalization of competitiveness and commerce

- Shifts to the use of web-based training for workers

- Shifts by the U.S. Army to distance learning via laptop computers

In 2000, students who could afford distance education had their choices of more than 6,000 accredited courses on the web. While 710,000 students enrolled in distance learning courses in 1998, more than 2 million students are expected to enroll in 2002 (U.S. Department of Education, Web-Based Education Commission, 2000, p. 77). According to a recent government document, the average distance learning student is 34 years old, employed part-time, has previous college credit—and is a woman (U.S. Senate, 2001).

Some call what is happening an educational revolution—the first major change in higher education in seven centuries (Cookson, 2000, p. 79). Those who argue that higher education has remained basically the same for many centuries ignore what, for women, has been a revolutionary change during the last century and half: The admission of women into colleges and universities has evolved from a statistical rarity to women slightly outnumbering men overall in undergraduate programs.

Online education should offer important new options and opportunities for women and men interested in higher education, courses, or degrees. Many promoters of web-based courses promise increased and improved educational opportunities, especially for the educationally disadvantaged, which can include adult students, single parents, and others who are unable to attend courses on campuses because of job and family responsibilities, health and physical limitations, or incarceration. However, technology-based changes in higher education programs will not automatically bring increased equality to everyone interested in and deserving of university courses and degrees. In fact, our technological history shows that, at least initially, the uses of new media mimic existing methodologies and disciplines (Brown, 2000, p. 12).

This report examines the convergence of two major trends: the growth of technology and distance education in the college and university setting, and the demographic shift toward a predominantly female population of non-traditional-age college students (60 percent of students over the age of 25 are women). It focuses on understanding why women pursue online education, what constraints they may face in doing so, and how they perceive online culture, social identity, and communications.

Why Ask Women About Distance Education?

In this study of gender and online education, we attempt to remedy the lack of attention paid to women's interests and involvement with online education by paying special attention to women's assessments of their experiences and concerns.

Why is attention to women's perspectives needed in distance education? First, women are the primary users of online education, yet they are dramatically underrepresented in the high-tech sectors charged with producing technological solutions and designing technological delivery systems, software, and educational packages. They are also underrepresented among college and university faculty and administrators currently shaping distance education.

Second, many women returning to college classes face significant barriers not usually experienced by men, or at least not experienced to the same degree. Many women balance job, community, and heavy family responsibilities against their academic work. They often have serious financial burdens. Traditionally they have grappled with these difficulties while also facing inflexible class schedules and academic policies, inadequate childcare, lack of appropriate housing, and lack of reliable transportation (Furst-Bowe, 2000). Can distance learning programs possibly alleviate some of these difficulties?

Finally, adult women often have been—and are today—targeted as a primary constituency for online learning. In the past century, women constituted the majority of students in correspondence courses. Educators usually thought of these women, if they were thought of at all, as education consumers working on the sidelines of higher education to fulfill individual goals. Now that distance education programs have evolved technologically and, under various social pressures, moved to the center of many university programs (at least in terms of long-

range plans), universities are searching not only for successful, cost-efficient online courses and programs, but also for additional students to take the courses. Adult women are recruited (although evidently not as consumers of computer science and post-graduate business courses and programs*), yet we know little about how these students and potential students feel about education or about how distance education may or may not increase their access to education.

Many of the women who participated in this study described themselves as having problems (e.g., not enough money to continue their education, many family responsibilities) that require them to improvise individual and often extremely difficult solutions. While their individual situations differ, the number of women currently working to complete courses and degrees online represents a social phenomenon. Awareness of women's problems and action to help overcome the problems are needed to increase the success of women and online programs.

A Brief Description of Methodology

This report is based on a study of interview and questionnaire responses from more than 500 women and men from many occupations, as well as a review of published research on distance learning (see the Appendix for a more complete description of methodology).

Given the increasing commitments of universities and individuals to the development of educational technology infrastructures and the relatively little information about gendered uses of technologies, we asked broad questions about the social and economic aspects of information and communication technologies in higher education. We expanded the discussion by listening to the ideas

---

*Advertising for some courses seems to be aimed at men. For example, a recent advertisement announcing a new online master's degree in business administration features a photo of a young **man** in a business suit carrying a baby and groceries. The text reads, "So you can get that degree you need to advance your career, without putting the rest of your life on hold" (*Smart Money*, Feb. 2001, p. 151).

and concerns of those *avoiding* distance technologies, as well as those profitably employing them.

Data were collected over a 16-month period using in-depth interviewing and an online questionnaire. Information was gathered from a total of 534 people (481 women and 53 men), including many women reentering academia, potential online students, and teachers and administrators interested in the possibilities and problems of online learning. The interview protocol and online questionnaire included questions about access to resources needed for online learning, learning styles, best and worst educational experiences, and experiences, worries, and successes regarding online education.

We conducted interviews in a variety of places, including homes, businesses, and schools. We collected, transcribed, coded, and analyzed data concurrently to develop theory, additional questions, and key observations as they emerged. Secondary sources provided information about related historical and contemporary actions and about research findings regarding gender and distance learning.

Because many of the most critical issues for women in online education are only now being recognized —and because our sample is, in part, self-selected rather than the product of a random-selection procedure—this study is not an appropriate candidate for quantitative (statistical) analysis. The focus in this study is on researching perspectives and recurring themes expressed by the respondents.

One caveat: any report dealing with computers and Internet use must recognize that statistics about online education change rapidly. Technological change is inevitable. While we recognize that there is always change, we also need to remind ourselves that early designs and decisions about structure and delivery can have long-lasting consequences. The emphasis in this study is, therefore, on long-term issues that have been largely ignored in research and on discussions about attitudes and practices on the Internet and in online education.

Part 2

Why Women Go Online:
Educational Plans, Preferences, and Aspirations

 Contrary to a perception that most online students pursue discrete skills-oriented courses for career or other pragmatic ends, women in this study reveal a wide range of motivations and goals for their online experience. Indeed most respondents are pursuing degrees and emphasize the personal enrichment of the experience as well as its utility. A smaller number pursue courses to meet career needs, while others take courses simply for the enjoyment of learning.

Educational Plans

Although women have varied backgrounds, most have clear visions of what courses and degrees they want and for what purposes. The surprise is, perhaps, how focused they are despite a dearth of clear information about accredited online courses and programs in comparison to traditional programs.

Summaries and examples of respondents' plans follow, beginning with the types of responses given most frequently by the 375 women answering the question about their reasons for taking online courses.

The degree-seekers

More than a third of the respondents are working on or plan to work toward a specific degree online. An almost equal number of these degree-seekers are working on associate, bachelor's, or graduate degrees. Many women underscore, however, that they value not only the credential, but also the personal enrichment and knowledge they acquire through online classes. They view personal and professional advancement as intertwined.

Some women seeking an associate degree define it as an intermediate step in a longer process of educational and occupational preparation. A 32-year-old rural carrier, for example, sees the associate degree as a means to "take out a business loan and open a retail store in a nearby location."

> *I am going to take advantage of courses through the U.S. Coast Guard. (I am the spouse of a member.) I plan to obtain my associate's degree, so that I can attend a state university. I would like to finish my master's degree by the time my children are in high school.*
>
> —Homemaker and freelance writer, 24, married, children at home

Several women seeking bachelor's degrees aspire to complete the entire degree online. "Distance ed will be part of my life," a flight instructor predicts. "I am already earning my bachelor's online and will try to do my master's the same way." A 37-year-old domestic engineer also wants to complete her bachelor's degree through distance education: "I want to have a home-based business, and set up programs in the community to help kids and their families."

Contrary to popular belief, students do not limit their online course-taking to specific vocational or training goals. Many women in this survey are completing or want to complete bachelor's and advanced degrees through distance learning, including a trainer who for years has been researching how to do her doctoral program online.

> *I would love to get a degree at some point, and every course I take, onsite or online, is toward that end. If I could complete my undergraduate education online, I would. [Taking classes] is for both personal and career gains, intertwined.*
>
> —Self-employed seamstress, 31, married, children at home

The pragmatists

Respondents in the second-largest group report that they are taking online classes, because they must do so to advance or develop their careers. These women generally offer briefer and less varied explanations than do the degree seekers described above. "I am using distance education right now to obtain a degree for career advancement. I don't think I could ever call this pleasure," a 49-year-old alumni director summarizes.

The reluctant users

Women in the third largest category indicate that they do not plan to take a distance education course, are not sure whether they would, or plan to use distance learning seldom or only under extenuating circumstances. "I would prefer not to but if I didn't have a choice I would try it," explains an outdoor educator. A grant writer emphasizes |that she might pursue an online course "if the opportunity presented itself from a reputable university."

> *I am planning on going to a tech school located 5 minutes down the street from my home [rather than take online courses]. ... It is away from home and it is close enough so I can still be available to my family but without having the distractions (sibling rivalry, household chores, phones ringing, etc.).*
>
> —Social worker, children at home

The lifelong learners

The fourth largest category includes women who pursue online courses primarily because they aspire to be lifelong learners, although, as one woman notes, "the outcome will also advance my career." Some state that they have obtained as many degrees as they want or need, and they enjoy online courses simply to satisfy their pleasure in learning. A technical instructor with distance learning experience explains: "I have my degree—but I hope to continue learning and growing as a person. Distance learning helps provide opportunities for education without tying me to a fixed location every week."

> *Although I only have a BA (in elementary education), I have no interest in further degrees. I am always thirsty for more understanding, knowledge, pleasure.*
>
> —Caregiver for grandchild and retired state legislator, 62

The interested poor

Some women are interested but "too poor right now to even consider" online classes, as a "divorced, poor, and stressed" woman describes herself. Others in this category specify that they cannot afford the computer and other course materials required for online learning.

Some women who had identified online programs of interest indicate that distance learning may solve time constraints but not financial constraints. A single, 55-year-old consultant survey designer states: "Online courses are usually overpriced given the relative cost of providing such instruction compared to onsite instruction. I resent the charges currently asked by many programs. ... I had hoped that the Internet would provide a more economical means of acquiring 'higher' education."

The career changers

Some women taking or interested in taking online course want to make their lives better for themselves or for themselves and their children. For some this goal means using distance learning to change career paths. A 22-year-old bartender plans "to use the education to become something—basically to get away from what I am doing. I do not want my mind to rot and I am ready for a career." Other women cite a desire to move toward a career that satisfies "monetary needs as well as emotional needs," as a medical radiology transcriptionist who feels "empty in my current field" explains.

The disappointed

More than a dozen women want to obtain a degree online but cannot find courses in their fields. "I already used online courses to finish my bachelor's degree," a 40-year-old executive assistant comments, "and I would use it again to get my master's degree. However, there is still a very limited number of degrees that you can get totally online/distance right now."

Preferences

Adult online students came of age in traditional classrooms—rooms with desks in rows facing a teacher's desk or a dais on an elevated platform. Even now, institutionally drab campus rooms are used in 50-minute sequences and are equipped with bells that begin and end the time that teachers and students spend together. Increasingly classrooms, at least in better-endowed colleges, are equipped with electronic teaching aids such as overhead projectors and connections for computers. While classrooms offer a place for students and teachers to meet on a regular basis with the possibility of stimulating conversations and challenging lectures, some students may experience the classroom and its rhythm and structure as confining, tedious, or unduly regimented.

Now that distance learning has created new means of delivery for education, we asked respondents whether they would prefer online or traditional classes.

Online courses

Almost half of the approximately 350 women who responded to this question opt for online courses, the vast majority for pragmatic reasons involving their current work and family situations. (Women responding to the online survey may be more likely to favor distance learning than a representative sample of women in school might be.) Dozens of women praise the flexibility of online courses, and many others cite the ability to control of their time and schedules. A much smaller number explain that they actually prefer the online learning experience itself.

Having flexibility

Flexibility—the ability to control their time and coordinate work, school, and home responsibilities —is a watchword for women who prefer online education and is a particularly strong selling point for adult women students who typically bear the brunt of family and work responsibilities. When it comes to education, time may be a more precious commodity than money for some of these women. A community college program director who has taken both types of classes prefers distance learning because it "allowed me to work on classwork on my schedule. ... I could take my laptop on business trips and work on classwork in hotels or work early morning hours or on the weekend. [I was] not locked into a specific class time/place."

> *The flexibility of submitting papers at midnight is critical to my accomplishment. Because I own my own business and am a wife and mother, I would have a more difficult time attending an on-campus class regularly and promptly.*
>
> —Marketing consultant, 40, married, child at home

Women who mention flexibility state that distance learning allows them to fit education into their work and family schedules, rather than trying to fit their lives into the schedules of traditional education. "I work full-time and have a family," a 43-year-old associate faculty member describes. "I must find courses in my doctoral program that fit my schedule. Pretty impossible at times!"

Learning at their own pace

Some women appreciate the flexibility of the online learning process itself and the ability to study at their own pace without schedule restrictions.

Explains a survey design consultant: "I like to learn at my own pace (fast) and at odd (to other people) hours. ... I often remain at the computer learning new software for 10+ hours at a stretch and prefer such intensive immersions vs. classrooms broken into hourly learning sessions." A 51-year-old director of communications similarly values the completion of courses "at a pace that is comfortable for me. I do not appreciate micromanagement either at work or in an academic situation."

> *Distance education, please! My own time, my own pace. I can go to my son's football games, I can see my daughter play basketball for the first time in her life. ... I can spend much-needed time with my husband. I can do my own thing, when I choose to do it— and still work ten hours a day! What more can you ask for!*
>
> —Air Force civilian, 37, married, children at home

Minimizing commuting costs and time

Some women prefer online education to save the time, costs, and hassle of commuting to colleges many miles away. A single, 38-year-old speech pathologist reports that with distance education she can spend more time studying rather than traveling 200 miles to the nearest college offering the courses she needs. A 35-year-old South Dakotan says that blizzards and hazardous conditions can make traveling 90 miles to the nearest college impractical.

Enjoying online courses

While most fans of online courses give pragmatic reasons, a much smaller number indicate that they substantively prefer online classes, some emphatically so. A teacher's aide praises the relaxed atmosphere of distance education, and an instructor with children at home prefers distance learning because she loves using the Internet. Other women value interaction with diverse students, including a teacher's assistant who has "contact with students from the West Indies, Japan, and Saudi Arabia" in her distance learning class.

Minimizing childcare costs

Many women mention that distance education helps them control childcare and travel costs, and some list these indirect costs as the primary reason for their online preference. "If I could cut my two-hour per day commute to classes, my life would be so much easier," explains a single mother who lives at home. "I pay $500 per month in day care fees so that I can go to school."

Meeting special needs

Women who wrote about physical problems and psychological characteristics in traditional classrooms also indicate in follow-up conversations that their special needs are rarely understood. Working online often alleviates problems of access associated with physical disabilities.

Traditional classroom

While women who have taken only traditional courses usually say that they prefer traditional education, many of them also say that they are interested in trying distance education courses. Many women who have taken both say they prefer traditional classes, but their situations make it impossible or difficult for them to take such courses. Women prefer traditional methods of instruction, in descending order of prevalence, for face-to-face interaction, the structured pace of the traditional classroom, better learning and retention, and immediate feedback from teachers and fellow students.

> *I prefer traditional ... but I did like certain aspects of distance learning because 1) it's at my pace, 2) I can zap off e-mail to the professor, and 3) Convenience and time savings in commuting. ... However, one disadvantage of distance learning is lack of interaction with professors and other students, and missing the classroom dialogue.*
>
> —Reference librarian, 52

Enjoying the interaction and social aspects of the classroom

Most women who prefer the traditional classroom point to its social atmosphere and face-to-face encounters. Significantly, these women view interaction online as a less satisfying, immediate, or authentic form of human contact than face-to-face contact. "I prefer being with live people over sitting in front of a computer alone," a high school English teacher comments. Another woman states that online instruction would not make her feel like a student. As an account executive says: "I recently had to choose between the two. I chose traditional because I would miss the human contact."

Many women who prefer the social aspects of the traditional classroom elaborate that they like to see facial expressions and other nonverbal responses and cues of classmates and instructors. "Traditional is best because you maintain face-to-face rapport with your instructor and classmates," says a 48-year-old teacher, who is working on a master's degree through distance learning. Another woman echoes, "Interactions with students and [seeing their] facial expressions can teach you a thing or two." A 39-year-old billing clerk characterizes distance learning as "very solitary, and much discipline is needed to keep yourself on track." She prefers traditional classes because they are "MUCH easier. You see the instructor face-to-face; you can freely ask questions, and you can listen to the questions raised by other students. [You can hear] ideas and thoughts you may not have envisioned on your own."

Needing the structure and pacing of the classroom

Just as some women prefer distance learning for the autonomy and self-pacing they feel it allows them, other women prefer the traditional classroom for its structure. A driving instructor admits that she "needs a structured environment and attention," and another respondent observes that she tends "not to do my best in distance education (just enough to get by)." A few of these women feel that the traditional classroom is a sterner taskmaster than the Internet, where they can "'blow off' the ... courses ... too easily," as a 42-year-old woman describes. A teacher confirms, "Traditional classroom makes

more demands on my efforts. Keeps me more on track."

Learning and retaining more through traditional classroom instruction

Some women feel that traditional instruction benefits them as "visual learners" and provides a "hands-on atmosphere [that] assists in material retention," as a computer lab technician elaborates. An office assistant notes that she has a learning disability that necessitates "hear[ing] and see[ing] instruction."

Wanting the possibility of immediate feedback and tutoring

Some women prefer the traditional classroom because they want immediate feedback. While distance learning may offer instant feedback, these women "feel more comfortable when I can ask questions or get clarification," as a technology coordinator summarizes. An airline employee writes, "[The] traditional method allows for immediate feedback and less time spent writing."

> *I took a distance course before, but I just prefer to have a body there giving instructions.*
>
> —High school counselor, 30, single, child at home

Combination of traditional and online methods

Respondents know that people learn in a variety of ways, and many refer to their own learning styles when they indicate whether they prefer traditional or online formats. Many state that they would most like a combination of formats. A 32-year-old woman prefers "traditional and would like this to be supplemented with an online component." This hybrid of traditional and online is increasingly what on-campus students experience today, as many of their classes use communication and information-gathering technologies via the Internet. A 46-year-old flight attendant and graduate student seeks "the input of peers in a conference table setting," yet feels that "distance education would certainly make life easier for me."

> *I prefer a combination of both. I live in a rural area ... the nearest college is one hour away. And I am a snowbird in the winter. With distance learning I could experience uninterrupted instruction—but it's nice to listen to a live person once in a while.*
>
> —Retired English-as-a-second-language teacher, 61

Several dozen women say that the preference for traditional or online learning would depend on the specific course. They argue that certain subjects may be more amenable to one or the other method. Some women prefer a traditional classroom if the subject is more technical, such as computer programming, but prefer distance education for a class such as English or math. A facility planner and manager prefers "distance education for all of my liberal arts/general education requirements," with traditional delivery for courses related to her field. A temporary employee and registered nurse says: "A course that involved theory, math problem solving, etc., I could learn with only occasional answers online. If it involved a 'hands on' subject like computer architecture, I would prefer traditional delivery." These comments challenge the perception that online education is valuable primarily for technical, non-liberal arts, skills-based subject matter.

A few others said that their preference would depend upon the skills and charisma of the teacher offering the courses. Many others stress that to even talk about the kind of instructional delivery and interaction they prefer is irrelevant, because they have no choice.

Comments
Most respondents who have taken online courses are generally enthusiastic about computer-based learning. This enthusiasm reflects that of students in a study done in the United Kingdom by Dewhurst, Macleod, and Norris (2000). Sixty-two students (76 percent of them women) in an undergraduate human physiology class used computer modules with color graphics and animation—tools that encouraged interactivity by, for example, requiring

students to drag labels from a list and drop them in the correct places on diagrams and to perform such calculations as pulse and vessel resistance. In general, students liked the flexibility offered by the computer-based program, which enabled them to study at their own pace and where and when they wanted. Another recent U.K. study found that most adult students taking part in (different-sized) online forums found the experiences positive (Hammond, 2000).

Other studies comparing online courses to traditional courses with similar content indicate that students can be equally satisfied with different methods of learning. One recent study found, however, that traditional students perceived that they had more interaction than did online students, even when a collaborative group project was included to promote online interaction. The online students indicated that they missed the face-to-face contact they would typically have in a traditional course, but the convenience of not having to drive long distances was more important than the contact (Card & Horton, 2000, pp. 241-242).

Many recent studies are primarily case studies with small sample sizes. They are also limited in that students typically prefer the course delivery method in which they participate. The studies indicate that while delivery methods differ, many students can be satisfied with each. A major lingering concern, however, is that many students do not feel they have a choice about the educational delivery method.

Regardless of what they most want, many women report that they must take online courses to successfully manage their other responsibilities. They repeatedly report the need to be close to home for family obligations. Some men also report that because of employment obligations they want to take courses online, and several remark that they cannot leave their families to travel to or stay on the campuses that have the desired degrees.

A 31-year-old salesclerk and part-time student gave a fairly typical response when she said: "I really prefer to learn through discussions, but right now we need to save money, and I need to stay home with my children. My husband would be in favor of distance education since I would be able to care for my children instead of putting them in day care."

An Education of Last Resort?

Participants were asked if they thought that distance education is a good alternative study method when it is the only way to take a course. Not surprisingly, almost all responded with at least an initial "yes." More than half stated that distance learning provides excellent opportunities for women who have children, heavy work responsibilities, disabilities, or tight schedules, or who reside in geographically isolated areas. "Internet learning is a dream come true for women like me with families and full-time jobs," a computer lab technician responds. A high school English teacher recommends distance learning because it "allows the caregiver to access a class at her/his convenience. For example, the quiet times for myself are after 11 p.m. when everyone is asleep. It is at this time I can concentrate."

Other respondents similarly characterize online learning as the educational option of last resort for some students who "may not have another chance to further their education," as a 34-year-old housewife describes. A 30-year-old with a child at home notes, "If the classes I took weren't online last semester, I would have dropped out of school for sure."

> *[Distance learning] allows us the option to continue growth during what could be inhibiting years.*
>
> —Program consultant, 52, married, child at home

Some women say that online programs are not only a viable last resort for women with tight schedules, but, even more explicitly, they also provide equal opportunities. "To deny an online education would be to deny education to someone based on a handicap. The handicap may be lack of transportation, childcare, or even a 'handicap' on the part of an institution [with] a limited number of faculty,

courses, and programs," opines a 51-year-old director of communications.

Best and Worst Experiences

Knowing what students think of as their best and worst educational experiences is an important basis for thinking about any major changes in higher education. What do women—or men—want from their education? What delivery methods, classroom styles, curricula, or other characteristics stand out in their minds as especially positive or negative? Hundreds of women were asked to assess their educational experiences and, significantly, most describe an online course as their best experience. Their recent educational experiences and the stated focus of this study undoubtedly produced more examples of online courses as best experiences than we would otherwise find. See the sidebar on pages 16 and 17 for the comments.

Learning Styles

Online courses use a variety of teaching and learning styles, and options will increase in the future, at least for those who can afford and wish to use computer microphones and cameras. Most respondents list more than one way when asked how they learned. Yet the highest number choose independent work because they have very tight schedules and they will receive grades based primarily on their individual work. The responses are listed from most to least frequently mentioned.

> *There are very few studies that look at the process of learning in online and distance education contexts, let alone the perspectives of the tutors and students involved.*
>
> —Vice president of education in a company that provides online tutoring and learning support, 38

Independent study is preferred
Challenging assumptions that women prefer to work in collaborative group settings, the majority of women indicate that they prefer independent

Educational Experiences Summary Statements

The following categories are listed from those given most frequently to those listed least often.

BEST

Individuals often indicate satisfaction with a combination of factors (e.g., teacher and teaching methods).

Experiences in online courses

"I am able to really spend time on any problems that I come across, and I have always been able to reach my professors by email, and they respond immediately."

—*Early childhood educator, 34*

"I am able to pursue my career and work full-time. I also have the opportunity to learn new technology."

—*Registered nurse, 25*

"The university people do their best to work with the soldier's hectic schedules. I was able to successfully complete the [online] course without the stress of [missing classes]."

—*Educational counselor, 35, single*

"One of the best classes I have taken. ... I had to go to the high school where the computer lab was networked [to the university]. You could see the teacher ... and she could interact with you. The atmosphere was relaxed and enjoyable."

—*Teacher's aide/student, 32, married, children at home*

Teachers

"My best educational experience was in college when an instructor allowed me into a class I didn't actually meet the requirements for but really wanted to take. He proved to me that I was not only a better artist/student/person than I had thought—but his faith in my strength and ability completely changed my perspective on life and molded the direction my future was to take."

—*Technical instructor, single, distance learning experience*

"My best experiences have always been associated with an open and caring instructor. ... Getting students involved and offering mutual respect always makes the experience valuable."

—*Professor, 49, single, child at home, distance learning experience as teacher and student*

"He was very active, candid, enthusiastic, and inspirational. ... This experience made me more aware of the need [in my own teaching] for demonstrations, labs, and hands-on experiences for the students."

—*High school science teacher, 29, married*

Subject matter

"Best experience—taking the leap of faith to leave a high-profile city job to follow my passion—that of herbs and herbal medicine. I began by taking a correspondence course and am now a third-year student at an herb school."

—*Herbalist/nutritional consultant, 35, single, distance learning experience*

Connections with other students

"For the last year I have been educated in teacher training by online distance learning and most of my fellow classmates are from various part of the world. Great discussion and brainstorming!"

—*Part-time student/full-time office administrative worker, 44, single, distance learning experience*

Teaching method and delivery

"I thought my education would suffer by taking classes outside the classroom. I was wrong. I've learned far more in my Internet courses than I had at many classes I took on campus. It's a lot of work and takes self-discipline, but I really enjoy being able to study and learn in the comfort of my own home and by my schedule."

—*Accountant, single, distance learning experience*

Personal Successes

"Acquiring my bachelor's degree at the tender age of 54 was intense but the day I was finally able to walk into graduate school was unimagined bliss. distance learning is a great boost to higher education, especially for women who still carry the duties of work as well as household. When we can use cable TV for a class, or, better yet, the Internet for a class, it is a real privilege."

—Salvation Army program director, 56, married, recent degree, distance learning experience

"[In the classroom} we were graded on pronunciation and the ability to captivate the class. I was granted the speech award for the year. Speech class taught me how to be expressive and free with my thoughts and emotions. A valuable lesson indeed."

—Homemaker, child at home, plans to work on master's online

WORST

Teachers

"I had a teacher (in graduate school!) who believed that it was his way or the highway and told us all that we couldn't possibly know anything about the subject except what we learned from him. It was the worst class I ever took."

—Conferences and events planner, 31, married

"I was an 'A' student in high school chemistry. ... No matter how much I enjoyed the study of [college] chemistry itself, I could not grasp anything that this man was teaching. ... I approached him after class with questions about what he had just covered and he would often reply with 'I just covered this in class.' After being humiliated so many times by him, someone who is supposed to offer support and assistance to the students, I gave up on chemistry altogether."

—Program aide in mental health, 24, single

"The professor who would effusively praise the one white male for anything he said and would discount any other comments from others in the class. It was discouraging."

—Associate professor, 42, married, children at home, has taught interactive TV course

Distance learning courses

"Worst, our online class. ... Our final project was a term paper and the due date had been posted. Somehow my instructor cut the class 5 days short. The problem was that everyone in the class got on the website only once a week. When he put on the site that the last quiz and the term paper were due 5 days early, at least half the class didn't see this posting until after the class had ended! He offered incompletes, but I need government reimbursement so I needed the grade that semester. He gave me my grade, but it was a lot of stress, and I received no apology."

—Student, 30, single, child at home

Costs

"I sometimes feel very punished for not wanting to be on welfare and making an active choice to seek and accomplish my education."

—Radiographer, 38

Boredom

"I never learn much when the instructor micromanages the class and has every assignment and project mapped out completely."

—Former software developer

Harassment and hostility in classes

"I was taking algebra and a classmate informed me that the instructor wanted to ask me out on a date. I decided to drop the class."

—Sales associate for luxury eyewear, single

Age

"I have found it very difficult to adjust to students' somewhat high school mentality such as grades for attendance."

—Sales/student, 31, married, children at home

study. Many had recently taken online courses, and online students may be more likely to prefer independent study. Older women may prefer different learning methods than do younger women, and technology and new communications methods may have changed students' expectations and preferences for education or make collaborative work more difficult.

While more than half list independent study as their first choice, many of them say they learn best by first reading, researching, and writing and then participating in group discussions to hear other opinions and ideas. "Independent work gets the knowledge available, the discussions implant it," a 22-year-old flight instructor explains.

> *I would choose a little of each, but if I had to rank them, I would put independent work first, followed by discussion, then group work. In group work, I tend not to be as self-assured as I should be. If someone in the group is pushy (even if they are not so competent), I will let them take over. I just do not enjoy the friction.*
>
> —Salvation Army program director, 56, married, recent degree, distance learning experience

Many women prefer independent study because they can count on themselves more than anyone else, an important factor for people with tight schedules. "I think the mature learner is usually on a mission, and independent work is fine," summarizes a high school guidance counselor taking an online course.

The best learning comes from a combination
Many women indicate that they learn equally, in integrated ways, from all three methods (group, independent, and a mix of both)—a "totality of elements," as an administrative assistant describes. A 30-year-old teacher states that she learns best from a combination: "We share ideas and expand our thinking through discussions. I go into deeper thinking and organize my comprehension through

independent work. In group work, we check our understanding and help fill each others' gaps." A 62-year-old retired state legislator reports that she relies on a variety of experiences: "I read, I listen, I ask, I feel, I experience; I need both group work and time to let ideas settle, sift."

> *I learn through discussion, independent [work], and group work. In any class you have independent work. The chat room discussions were just like being in a class situation (my typing is improving), and our study group via e-mail and chat room was a great learning tool.*
>
> —Educator, 52, married, finishing master's degree online except for field project

Group discussion is important
A smaller number of women indicate that they learn primarily through group work, because they are team players, accommodating-style learners, or socially outgoing. A grant writer, 62, for example, reports that she gets sidetracked easily, so discussions are usually the most efficient way to learn. She particularly likes short, intensive, focused workshops and seminars where teacher/student roles are flexible and interchangeable.

No group work, please!
Echoing women who express a preference for independent study, many women state that they loathe group work. Their reasons usually have to do with the difficulty of fairly allocating and sharing work. "I am a fairly organized, reliable, punctual person and I get upset easily with people who are laid back," comments a 28-year-old homemaker with children at home. A computer lab technician finds group work "fun but it can also be stressful if I am teamed with students who are not responsible."

> *Partners are notorious for letting people down; in my case I'd rather do it myself.*
>
> —Unemployed, 51, married, uses a wheelchair

Women also dislike group work because of the difficulty in agreeing on tasks and methods, logistical problems, pressure to go along with decisions made by the most powerful of the group, dislike of the indecisiveness and politics that can be involved in group work, and the relatively slow speed of group work. Many women reported enjoying group discussion but not group work.

Teachers are more likely than students to be interested in including group work in their courses.

The E-Student: Who Is Most Suited for Online Education?

Published guides for successful distance learning include the following student indicators for success in online courses: highly motivated, independent, active learners who have good organizational and time management skills, study without external reminds, and adapt well to new learning environments (see, for example, *The Distance Learners Guide* [1999]). Women's descriptions of the ideal e-student confirm many of these characteristics.

Women responding to questions about the people most suited for online education mention both the pull factor (being interested in online learning because of the particular attractions of this method of studying) and the push factor (barriers to access to other methods of studying). Many note that success online depends on motivation, time-management skills, maturity, and, according to a smaller number of women, the ability to work late at night or early in the morning. Many of the respondents said that online courses are more likely to be a good fit for older women who are more focused on goals and less on social interaction.

Desirable student characteristics
Dozens of women believe that many students are well-suited for distance learning courses. Some argue that all classes should be available through distance education. The following characteristics are listed from the most to the least stressed. Summary statements describing which students are best suited for distance learning are included in the sidebar.

Students Best Suited for Distance Learning

"Those who work full-time and want to spend more time in their home environment. Those who are not confident about contributing in a classroom environment. Students with transportation challenges. Students who feel their family members can [support] them ... people who travel a lot and would miss too many classes, but who have access to a portable computer. Students who are homebound with young children. Students who have medical problems. ... Students who require privacy. Students who live in areas that have harsh winters ... etc., etc., etc."

—*Executive secretary, 56, married,*
distance learning experience

"Those who are not afraid of computers. ... Those who enjoy learning. ... Women who have families but don't want to put their educational pursuits on hold until children have reached maturity. Minority students. ... Students who write well and can do independent research."

—*Psychologist, 41, married, children at home,*
distance learning experience

"Those who are independent, highly motivated, have ideas of his/her own, are curious, willing to be open about life experiences and perceptions that may be counter-culture, or maybe someone who is isolated (social, emotional, familial, geographic) who wants to explore new options."

—*Grant writer, 62, married*

Highly motivated

Many women describe difficult situations in their lives where they saw education as the only way out. Distance learning provides a no-frills, direct route to an educational goal for the student who has "set her mind to doing it," a 43-year-old student observes. "I was just looking to the goal" of finishing a bachelor's degree, comments a 40-year-old executive, "not to the social interaction of it."

> *I was a run-away wife; I left a bad situation, with my daughter and my son. There's definitely a need for distance learning because there are a lot of other women of color like myself. I was living in St. Croix. After a major hurricane, the island was really crippled. I had a computer but no electricity. So for three months, I borrowed a generator in order to type my dissertation. It was a challenge, but I really wanted the degree.*
>
> —University teacher, 45

According to a 22-year-old flight instructor, highly motivated students are fed up with the traditional discriminatory attitudes of the standard classroom or don't have time to sit in a classroom learning materials that have no relevance to their daily or future life.

Women emphasize that primary caregivers may have special incentives to excel at distance learning. A nail technician and single mother taking two online classes believes that distance learning is best suited to "people like me who have no choice but to work to make ends meet but want to go to school so they won't have to struggle for the rest of their lives."

Independent

Most of the women taking online courses think of themselves as being or becoming independent students and stress the importance of this trait for online success. Significantly, although most online courses include chat rooms or forums for discussion, respondents often characterize online education as solitary pursuits that reward "a person who is comfortable working alone, not needing direct social contact with others," as a 28-year-old student observes. A 36-year-old paralegal suggests that the student most suited for online courses "does not thrive on being with people all the time."

Older, more mature students or non-traditional-age students

Some women mention maturity and view older, more experienced students or non-traditional-age students as beneficiaries of online courses. A 52-year-old program consultant talks about how many women of her era are experiencing the four Ds—death, downsizing, drug and alcohol abuse, and divorce. But, she notes, these women are also using technology to support themselves through these otherwise isolating changes. If done right, she says, online courses can be exciting—and students can feel like there is a campus. Some women suggest that older students who took courses in a traditional classroom years ago may now have economic or physical reasons to consider distance learning.

> *What kind of student benefits the most from online learning? Probably people like me who are older. I would not feel as comfortable in a classroom of all young people.*
>
> —Unemployed, 49, married, no distance learning experience

Conversely, a few women mentioned that distance education might work well for high school students who wish to take courses not offered in their schools or who are academically ready for college but not ready for the college "experience."

Good computer skills

Some respondents mention the need for good computer skills.

> *What student is best suited? The visually oriented student because you need to be doing hands-on work, interactive with the computer.*
>
> —Teacher, 39, married, children at home, taking graduate courses online

Ambitious

Some women stressed the importance of drive, focus, and a passion for learning, all closely related to motivation. For example, an environmental technician feels that the distance learning student "needs to have a serious education goal in mind ... and not just [be interested] because he/she won't have to get up and attend a traditional class at 8 a.m."

> *Ambitious, goal-oriented, independent thinkers who will seek out the resources needed to complete assignments.*
>
> —Former software developer/graduate student, 33, married, child at home

Other characteristics

The student most suited for distance learning has financial and emotional support from others at home; the desire for material relevant to the student's daily or future life; a willingness to embrace challenges; good communications skills; good typing skills; an enjoyment of written communications, perhaps even over the spoken word; a willingness to work harder than students taking courses in the classroom; a lack of access to traditional classroom courses; and physical disabilities that make classroom attendance difficult.

Comments

We asked the respondents to focus on the attributes of individual students. We could also, with benefit, have asked what characteristics an online program must have to make it possible for students to study effectively and finish courses successfully. Based on the information in this report, one possible response is the ideal educational experience provides students with a variety of different learning opportunities (an integrated system of online time, lectures, collaborative sessions, one-on-one interactions with a peer or professor), considers employment and family responsibilities, and offers courses at a cost that reflects not only institutional costs but also the resources of students.

Part 3

The Digital Divide:
Gaps and Bridges

 Increasingly, distance learning or online education means accessing educational material through the Internet, so research on how various social and economic groups use the Internet is relevant to any study of online education.

> *There's "an information caste society"—a two-tiered system, a wired population and a population that isn't. The reason the caste metaphor fits is that the division is highly self-perpetuating. For example, people who are online know which programming languages are still important for jobs. People who aren't online are making decisions based on outdated information.*
>
> —Nicholas Burbules, university professor and educational technology researcher

The initial euphoria over the Internet resulted from its democratic potential and environment. This electronic space did not see race, sex, socioeconomic class, or age, and thus admitted everyone as equals. Studies in the 1990s, however, sounded cautionary notes that access to and use of computers varied greatly depending upon class, age, nationality, race, and native languages. These studies led educators and policy-makers to recognize a digital divide in education and online culture.

Yet in searching for factors that distinguish and explain the digital divide, researchers often ignore gender and focus exclusively on race/ethnicity, class, or region. In many digital divide discussions little mention is made of the differences between women and men overall or in any racial or ethnic group.

In addition, most surveys do not seek information about gender differences within households. We know that "family" resources often are not evenly divided among males and females in a household, so studies that treat the family as one unit of analysis do not give us information about computer ownership and use *within* the family.

Most surveys of Internet users pay attention to the socioeconomic and employment status of the users but do not ask the women and men respondents questions about, for example, work and family responsibilities—and thus about time and financial factors that may be centrally responsible for the purchase, maintenance, and use of computers.

This section will explore potential obstacles that women identify to online participation.

Student Costs

Students and prospective students discussed costs of education more than any other topic. Many people remain convinced that distance learning eventually will be a relatively inexpensive mode of education. Many women with difficult economic situations express keen interest in taking courses; however, at the moment distance learning is used disproportionately by the relatively well-resourced. Some poorer students may take a course and then temporarily drop out of the program to earn and save money to pay for the next course, trying to earn a degree even if it takes many years.

Understanding the full costs of education also requires understanding indirect costs and, for women, inequalities of power, resources, and access in families. For example, respondents indicate that the cost of childcare usually is added to women's lists of expenses but not to men's. Successful students report that family members support them. But many report heavy home demands, which often make it difficult for them to take and complete distance education courses.

> *[Money is] always the issue. My husband lost his business at 52, and at 59 sees the company he is working with going under. I have been looking for funding but have no good leads. I had to borrow from family for my last two classes. I feel like quitting because I'm adding such a burden with money we don't have.*
>
> —Elementary school teacher, 56, married, distance learning experience

Tuition

Most students report paying approximately the same tuition for online classes as they do for traditional courses. The debate about institutional costs for different delivery methods continues, with some recent reports indicating that online instruction is usually more expensive than in-person instruction, at least for courses without many sections (Carr, 2001).

In the past, only those students taking at least 12 hours of traditional courses a week could be considered full-time and apply for federal full-time financial aid. (This regulation was enacted in part to prohibit federal financial aid to mail order diplomas or diploma mills.) Financial aid is not a major concern for working men and women whose companies cover their educational expenses, but it is a huge concern for millions of single parents with low incomes and no other financial resources. More than one third of college students attend classes part-time; more than half of these students take fewer than six credit hours each term (Wolff, 2001).

Funding for distance learning may be more limited or restricted than for traditional courses. Several women comment that restrictions on funding and loans for distance learning impede their participation. "I have a child and a job and I looked at the possibility of taking online courses, but the main reason that I did not ... was because the financial aid ... would not cover any costs, and I just did not have that kind of money," observes a graduate student and online tutor in her 20s.

While their specific situations and accounts vary, single women without children often mention that they can afford to take a course because they are single. They speculate that they would not have as much financial freedom or time if they had complex family responsibilities.

> *If I wanted to take a distance-learning course, I'm sure my agency would find a way to pay for it. Or, I would not have much of a problem affording a class myself, from time to time. My lifestyle is not constrained by demands of a family, work schedule, and financial well-being.*
>
> —Family transportation specialist, 23, single

In this study women who responded to the questions about online education do not represent a random sampling of U.S. women. They do, however, come from an impressive variety of occupations, experiences, and economic situations. Many of them report difficult financial situations even as they strategize to find ways to take online courses. In this they are similar to the women in a number of other studies that found the cost of education, including distance education, a particularly difficult barrier for women to overcome (Blum, 1998).

> *Cost is the most important factor. I am a homemaker. My husband is not very supportive of my pursuing a degree. I currently have no income of my own. ... Most agencies do not seem to provide grants to individuals seeking education via distance learning.*
>
> —Homemaker/former financial director, married, children at home

In some cases distance education may be more expensive than traditional courses. "The cost of some of the online courses I have researched has prevented me from taking advantage of them," comments a 40-year-old single woman with children at home. "I've found distance education courses more expensive than traditional. By the time I complete my degree, I will have paid the same amount of money as a student who went to a four-year college with housing, books, and tuition." This woman also flags a potential indirect cost if an online course is not approved or cannot be applied toward her degree program, thus necessitating further courses and tuition costs.

Computer-related costs

Some respondents either do not own a computer or own a computer that is inadequate for online courses. Conflicts among family members over computer use usually do not appear in studies that assess household use of computers. For example, a guidance counselor explains that to take an online course, "We might need a new computer at home. We all use it so much I would have to 'fight for time' on the machine."

Students point out that for online courses they are expected not only to know how to use computers, but also to have Internet access (Selfe, 2000, April). While not all of them own a computer, most manage some access to the Internet. Some have access to computers, e-mail, and the Internet through their workplace and do not pay direct costs; others use community freenets or commercial services that charge a standard monthly or hourly rate. These costs and resources need to be considered in addition to tuition when thinking about who has access to online learning.

Students also face unique financial and technological pressure with upgrades and improvements to their computer systems.

> *Constantly, it seems, there are new [software] versions. And then if you don't purchase this or don't upgrade to that, then you have other things that you find on the Internet that won't run because you need the newer versions. ... Plus the computer itself seems to [be outdated] in about two years. Not only do you have to figure out how to get money for new ones, you have to figure out what to do with the old ones.*
>
> —Teacher, 34

Students using online resources may find that tuition and access to computer equipment are not the only expenses. For example, several companies offer fee-based online access to books and journals to help students write papers more quickly without trips to the library. (Much of the material most useful for research papers, including book texts, may not be available through such services, raising other pedagogical issues.) Some faculty are concerned that this situation will perpetuate a division of have and have-not users, and faculty consequently encourage these companies to promote institution-wide site licenses to give all students access to the services (Blumenstyk, 2000).

Childcare expenses

Some mothers state that they save money overall by taking online courses and avoiding childcare costs, which offset the higher or comparable tuition costs of online courses. An instructional assistant found online and on-campus tuition costs comparable, but she has a "special needs child at home and [doesn't] have many childcare options" and, therefore, chose the online course.

Global concerns

Women in other countries list many of the same problems mentioned by women in the United States. Tuition was the central concern for almost all. Additional major problems were difficulty of access to computers and to the Internet, unreliable electrical sources, difficulty finding good online programs in their own culture or language, and difficulty obtaining academic journals and books in nearby libraries.

Age as a Classroom Issue

The ages of typical undergraduate and graduate students have been rising. In recent years, adult undergraduates 24 years of age or older represented between 40 and 45 percent of college students (U.S. Department of Education, National Center for Educational Statistics, 1997). Just 16 percent of college students now fit the traditional college student profile: 18-22 years old, attending school full time, and living on campus (U.S. Department of Education, Web-Based Education Commission, 2000, p. 4).

A large percentage of adult students (65 to 70 percent) are women (Donaldson, Graham, Martindill, & Bradley, 2000, p. 9), however, many older women students perceive themselves to be anomalous or different on campus. Many respondents indicate that because they are older than the typical college student, they feel more comfortable online than on campus.

> *Because of my age (31), compared to the average college student (18-19), I feel I don't need the social aspect as much as someone younger may feel they need it. In fact, on some levels, I'm happy not to have to deal with other students.*
>
> —Legal secretary, 31, distance learning experience

Some women note that they are more comfortable asking questions and conversing online with women closer to their own age because they relate emotionally. "The young teachers are just as willing to help, but it makes me feel old and stupid," says a 56-year-old.

Similarly, a number of women list age-related experiences in the traditional classroom as factors in their worst educational experiences. For example, a 59-year-old high school teacher describes her worst experience in a core math course where she was unable to follow the lessons quickly: "I would not question anything because I was embarrassed because I was probably the oldest student in the class and felt that I should have been able to keep up."

A self-employed seamstress who attended traditional courses at a university finds herself frustrated: "I don't have the open exchange of ideas and general fellowship with other students that I felt right out of high school. There is a lack of commonality and empathy that I feel is a barrier in classrooms of mixed ages. I wish it could work. In an ideal world it would, but in my personal experiences, it just hasn't."

> *At 37 years of age, a mother [of seven children], a wife, a career woman, I am not worried about what I am missing in a classroom. ... In fact, I'd be reluctant to attend an on-campus class today, especially considering my age.*
>
> —Air Force billing clerk, 39, single, child at home, distance learning experience

Some older women welcome the relative anonymity of online culture: "Because we could not visually see each other ... we did not have preconceived ideas about backgrounds [or] abilities. I found that to be interesting. ... Most did not know that I was 55+ unless I told them."

Age issues in the future

Several administrators predict that evaluations of online and traditional courses will change as U.S. children, raised with TVs and computers in their homes and in their classrooms, enter universities and colleges. Administrators, teachers, and students who participated in the study agree that by the time today's elementary school students are eligible for college and university, they will be comfortable using computers as educational tools. Some of the teachers indicate that college-age men who are accustomed to computer action games find text-based online courses slow and dull.

> *One of the evaluations that came back had one of our instructors as being more effective over video than when he was live. ... I expect that among younger learners that this [video-conferencing] would be a more natural way to learn because they've all grown up with television, and computers are such a big part of their lives.*
>
> —Senior information technology adviser, male, 26

The silent online majority?

Older women who report being comfortable with computers and interested in online courses are surprised to hear about similar students. But how would they know? Not through media images, which rarely show older women competently using computers. In TV commercials, for example, female computer users are rarely over 40, and girls are seen much less often than boys. When women are shown using computers, it is usually for routine, unremarkable activities, while men are more likely to be shown embracing the technology for more enjoyable activities, such as playing games (White & Kinnick, 2000, p. 406).

Respondents suggest that they worry about being old or older students at remarkably young ages. Students in their late 20s think of themselves as being unusually old. Not only do women out-number men among older students, research suggests that women worry about age differences in the classroom to a much greater extent than older male students (American Association of University Women Educational Foundation, 1999). While we hear of a lot about the importance of lifelong learning, universities have not actively demonstrated that students of all ages are welcome on campus and online. People of different ages will, of course, have somewhat different needs and concerns, so welcoming students of all ages will require changes in some programs.

Time Demands

The refrain that distance learning is a good option —or compromise—for women with children and little free time runs throughout this study. A few men also mention the value of distance learning for men with family responsibilities, but male and female respondents note that women, in particular, face time pressures when seeking education.

Women enrolled in online courses have even less time to call their own than do most students in traditional learning environments. Many of them serve a first shift at work outside the home and a second shift as primary caretakers of family members. The only way they can accomplish a third shift—their education—is to fit it in when and where they can. Women, especially those with children, have less free time to be away from their family responsibilities and other work. Distance learning allows them to study at home (at least in the evenings or when off work) while still performing home duties and being available when needed.

Institutions historically have been more concerned with separating the public, linear, formal work world than integrating the traditionally repetitive, multi-tasking, "feminine" world and its rituals of the household, childrearing, and the private sphere. (If institutional concerns were different, we long ago would have set up educational systems with schedules, costs, and provisions that more equally served workers with diverse demands.) While this view is admittedly overly dichotomized (most public leaders must also be available for many tasks at the same time), men and women who want to advance in their careers usually must demonstrate their commitment to their jobs through autonomy from their personal responsibilities (Woodward & Lyon, 2000).

The need to hide private responsibilities is particularly important for women who want to advance in their careers by taking courses and degrees while still maintaining familial relationships. Distance learning courses can be particularly valuable for women who can thus more easily pass the availability tests at work and at home.

As they discuss trade-offs they make in carrying out (often enjoying, sometimes resenting) family responsibilities and pursuing career goals, many women respondents express satisfaction that distance learning allows them to do several tasks at once.

Student time

Many online students mention enjoying online discussions but fervently wish to do assignments independently.

> *I am pretty busy just like my classmates and I really want to do the work [on my own] and not keep track of my group members.*
>
> —32-year-old social worker, distance learning experience

Most mothers study during late evening hours, or, less frequently, very early morning hours. Given that most of these women also have part- or full-time jobs, their preference to set their own study schedules does not seem surprising. One study found, however, that men in online courses usually study from 4 to 8 p.m., while most women studied later, presumably fitting in their course work after fulfilling other commitments (Richardson & French, 2000, p. 305).

While students praise the flexibility of distance learning, some studies show that students often find electronic course discussions time-consuming, especially those students who also meet face-to-face on campus during regularly scheduled times. Online courses may also accelerate the student's expectations about access to a professor's time and instant responses to questions. One study found that students appreciated their e-mail communication with an instructor who promised to return all messages within 24 hours (Chapman, 1998).

Most students who have taken online courses mention receiving quick e-mail responses from their professors, but some perceive a trade-off between speed and quality. "The only shortcoming I feel with my online classes was the lack of specific feedback from the instructor on assignments," complains a 59-year-old registered nurse. "I missed the instructor's comments in the margin. ... Feedback in the distance format seemed to be more global in nature. But this situation can change as instructors get more feedback from the students, and learn more about what technology has to offer."

One interviewee, a journalist who specializes in online education, notes that he had talked to many students who were frustrated because "there was never a classroom where they could get a quick answer."

Faculty time

The administrator of an accredited and very successful (in terms of retention and student satisfaction rates) online graduate degree program states that faculty in the program are given a full term (with no other courses to teach) to develop a new online course and are responsible for only one course the first term they teach it. Another online network administrator indicates that because online faculty at his university spend so much time supporting and advising students, they earn an extra thousand dollars per course. He also suggested that if online programs do not adequately support faculty, "nobody will want to teach these courses, because they're just too labor intensive."

Coordinating collaborative web-based courses is time-consuming for faculty members, particularly if they try to monitor the interaction in small group discussions that are a part of many web-based courses. Their continual involvement seems to discourage harassment (especially in undergraduate courses) and help guide and support discussions. These factors suggest that web-based courses need to be much smaller than many of the large lecture courses now offered in traditional programs. One study of the value of collaborative learning online for a master's in business administration program suggests that unless a college is prepared to commit substantial new resources to online programs, developing web-based courses and programs is not a good idea (Arbaugh, 2000, p. 508).

Comments

Most respondents emphasize that time is a critical issue for almost everyone involved in online learning. Students can overload teachers and vice versa. Students may expect very quick electronic responses to their individual requests and may create huge volumes of text in electronic discussions. Teachers can (too) easily, with a few keystrokes, send massive amounts of reading material to students (Hawisher & Moran, 1997). As one administrator for a center for new designs in learning and teaching warns, some teachers are "including a bunch of technological stuff but not taking anything out of the course to make room for it." Students may find themselves working more with the technology than with the professor or the subject material.

Family Factors

Online courses and programs are sometimes presented as the ideal higher education delivery methods for women, who are often assigned or take on most of the responsibilities for childcare and domestic work. In the United States, women still perform 70 to 80 percent of childcare, which, of course, affects how much time they can spend on paid work and education (Williams, 2000). The mismatch between the realities of family life and images of the ideal worker and student is a widespread social dilemma that, in Williams' words, is "bad for men, worse for women, and worst for children," with important implications for everyone in our country. Because it is seldom discussed as such, however, women are left to work out individual solutions.

> *We are made to feel guilty if we go to school when we "should" be taking care of children. Our government is not really interested in children or in education. If there was real interest, then the officials will begin by asking what is best for all human beings? What systems do we need to make things work the best? We would not start by saying, "Oh, online education is great for women who have to take care of children." Listen to the assumptions behind that statement.*
>
> —Graduate student, 40s, children at home

Lack of family support for online education may come in the form of increasing demands for attention and help, destroying course materials, guilt-tripping, denying childcare assistance, refusing to set aside time or space in the home for study, and refusing to spend family finances on women's education (Kirkup & von Prümmer, 1997; Campbell, 1999/2000, p. 32). Although some spouses at least verbally approve of course-taking, even this support often diminishes as women's study demands increase. (See Home [1998] for a discussion of role strain among women students.)

Few researchers have studied the ways women handle the multiple responsibilities of income provider, parent, and student. A Canadian study asked women re-entering college about their uses of institutional support such as distance education, day care, assignment date flexibility (during times of family crisis), study skills workshops, teacher accessibility, part-time study, study leave, access to computers at work, and employer reimbursement of educational expenses. Distance education was the institutional support most likely to reduce women's susceptibility to strain and overload (Home, 1998).

Other studies found that mothers often felt that they needed to reassure their families that their studies would have minimal impact on family life and that they felt guilt about not performing their domestic roles as well as before (Maynard & Pearsall, 1994). In a small qualitative research study in New Zealand, women participating in adult education kept evidence of their learning hidden from others in their families so the home was undisturbed by their student lives (Stalker, 1997). Because women receive little social or institutional support for taking courses once they have home and childcare responsibilities, women generally place higher demands on themselves to compensate for perceived selfishness when they pursue educational goals (Campbell, 1999/2000, p. 32).

In this study, women with spouses and children indicate that they would need, or want, to talk with their partners about taking an online course because of the costs and the time involved. Many men also indicate that they would want to talk with their partners before signing up for an online course. Most men with families, however, consider family responsibilities to be at their discretion.

> *My wife could[n't] care less if I decided to go back to school. ... However, I try to take into consideration that she has the baby full time and in the evenings plus the weekends. She needs a break, so I would consider planning around her schedule. Besides, I want to be a parent, too, and not leave it all to her.*
>
> —Computer programmer, 25

On the other hand, when asked whether they felt guilty or would feel guilty taking courses when there was other work at home, approximately half the women respond that they do not or would not feel guilty, even though many of them admit that their family responsibilities come first. Many try to do their course work while other family members are sleeping, or they postpone taking courses until their children are older and more independent. Other women couch their responses in terms of family interests, indicating that their continuing

education work is as important as other responsibilities, not only for themselves but also for other family members.

Some women report that because of circumstances beyond their control (such as a child's serious illness), they sometimes are unable to finish a course even though they are doing well. To them the term "drop out" (which they feel implies a failure on the part of the student) does not indicate the varying reasons a student may not complete a course in the allotted time. They argue that they may be *required* to leave their courses, because online programs and teachers usually have specific and restrictive deadlines for completion of all work, regardless of what may be happening in the students' lives.

Below are some of the women's responses to the question about whether they have felt or would feel guilty taking online courses. These responses make it clear that setting educational goals and priorities is a complex, continually changing task, especially for women with children and partners. The responses are listed from most to least frequently mentioned.

Guilty or not
As one might expect, children, especially young children, are the greatest impediment and heaviest responsibility for female distance learners. "No guilt," a counselor responds. " I have had to put off doing work at home ... to finish my coursework. My time is mostly my own and my daughter's." In contrast, a married woman responds: "I wouldn't feel guilty, but my husband would think differently. If he could see the direct connection in future income ... but he's under so much personal stress right now. I go home and [study] and he freaks out because he wants to sell the house and it needs cleaning."

A few women retort that they don't feel guilty because other family members and children can and should take on some family responsibilities. "Two other people live here, and they are not disabled in any way," notes a 44-year-old purchasing agent.

A police dispatcher similarly responds, "My son is old enough to handle some things on his own."

> **It's not a problem for me because I'm a single parent and my youngest child will graduate from high school in a few years and is very busy with her own activities. [Things were different] ten years ago when I had young children and a husband to deal with.**
>
> —Kitchen designer, 49, single

A 52-year-old disability specialist whose adult daughter is a new mother with health problems reports feeling "guilty if I pursue my own needs, and she feels guilty because assisting her prevents me from doing so." A technology coordinator who would feel guilty about taking a course says, "I would have to discuss it with my husband and son, as doing this would [require me to] rely on their help with my daughter."

Fitting in online education

Most single women and women with partners but no children say that they have more freedom than other women do. A human resources representative who is single explains, "I'm not obsessed with dust bunnies and at this point I don't have kids."

Typically, women report feeling more conflicted about neglecting time with their children than ignoring household tasks or chores, since in one woman's terms, "pursuit of my degree ranks higher in importance" than laundry. Single mothers feel less guilty about neglecting housework than do married women.

Others know that taking online courses would be especially difficult because of expectations that family members have about how women spend their time at home. For example, a 38-year-old substitute teacher says: "My husband and kids did make me feel guilty, because every time they turned around I was studying. When your child says, 'but you're ALWAYS studying,' it doesn't feel good."

Many women avoid guilt by making sometimes quite heroic efforts to slot schoolwork unobtrusively into their family and work schedules or by foregoing leisure time to accommodate their families and jobs. A single mother studies at midnight because she can't study with home responsibilities lingering. A 32-year-old social worker "studies after [she has] put the kids to bed ... [they] come first." Says a student with children at home, "I have learned to map out time either early in the morning or late at night." A self-described night owl enjoys online courses because they are "conducive to late-night study habits ... and I can spend quality time with my family before the children's bedtime." And a 39-year-old billing clerk feels guilty when "I am unable (or too tired) to complete assignments when my son sleeps."

> **I set aside two to three hours nightly to "catch up" on work and school-work so as not to interfere with my family life.**
>
> —Nursing recruiter/coordinator, 27, married, children at home

Many women indicate that the third shift of student life occurs late at night or early in the morning. While distance learning allows women to squeeze their studies around the seemingly immovable barriers of family and work life, this evades any general social discussion of how time and responsibilities, both in the work force and the home, might be reconfigured to make fulfillment of educational goals a more humane and less taxing process. Instead, women make individual compromises and choices—as family members, workers, and students—to fit all of these activities into short days. While an insomniac lauds late-night studying as "the beauty of online education," other women accustomed to more regular hours report that the third shift of education cuts into their already-scarce hours of leisure or sleep time.

Sticking to the schedule

In a related set of responses, women discuss the importance of self-discipline and family schedules as a corrective to guilt or feeling overwhelmed. Ostensibly distance education, which can occur within the household, should alleviate family-school tension and schedule conflicts. Yet women make clear that in some ways online learning requires more self-discipline and scheduling to maintain a space within the household for studying and learning. Since this space is not clearly demarcated by a specific class time and location on campus that requires a student's physical presence, women may find it harder to maintain a study schedule with distance learning, or at least may not find it substantially easier.

> *I am having trouble juggling all my work and school. In distance learning, you have to set aside the time you would normally be in the classroom, and devote it to your schoolwork.*
>
> —Single parent, 35

A few responses reveal fault lines in the allocation of tasks within the household, as women try to avoid relying on spouses and kids to carve out long, uninterrupted personal work times. Several women describe the importance of learning to budget time and knowing how to "get [housework] done in record time ... to give myself more time for my school work," as a 24-year-old homemaker describes.

A few women in this group maintain family schedules that everyone upholds. Says a 31-year-old legal secretary with a child at home: "I go by a schedule and check off things as they are done. I include home, work, and school deadlines. You must also prioritize."

Online learning: a family affair

Since distance education in effect brings the classroom into the home, it can involve family members in a variety of ways. Several dozen women note the importance of receiving active support and encouragement from partners and children, and several mention that they receive technical help from their partners as well.

Even when other family members are supportive, however, women indicate that they remain the person primarily responsible for household and family-related tasks. A 42-year-old woman describes her husband's household contribution, for example, as pitching in when needed. "My husband is very supportive of anything that I want to do. There would be no complaining from him if the laundry weren't done or the dishes were stacked up," says a 51-year-old director of communications. A part-time career counselor enjoys similar support from her husband who "helps me and very seldom complains about my classes, as he wants to take an online class" as well. A 25-year-old sometimes feels guilty about her class but notes, "My husband encourages me to go to school, so he has taken on anything that I don't have time to do."

> *My family rates above schoolwork, but they do understand if I need some extra time. My sons and I do homework together.*
>
> —Early childhood educator, 34, married, children at home, distance learning experience

A number of respondents report receiving passive support from spouses, for example, not being interrupted a lot while they are studying or not being made to feel guilty. "I feel no guilt because [my husband] does not present any," declares a 26-year-old distance learning student.

A matter of priorities

Several dozen women state that their children are their highest priority. But these women sometimes modify their statements by adding an assurance that classes are most important—after their family's needs. "Being head of the household I always have responsibilities at home," explains a retail manager. "It's a matter of discipline (which I must admit I haven't fully mastered) to set schooling as a higher priority than other work. My children's needs come first. ... Having a specific time every day to study helps, preferably when they're at school."

While most women with children at home prioritize attention to the family over coursework, some women list family as their first or only concern when asked whether they felt guilt. "I wouldn't feel bad because I would finish my family duties first," comments a 28-year-old married woman.

For the good of the family

Women who respond that they view education as something that advances their family's well-being typically do not feel guilty about pursuing online classes. They reconcile time away from the family by recognizing that further education may serve a family's long-term interests. "My guilt works the other way," responds a 30-year-old administrative assistant and single mom, who reports feeling guilty when, as the head of the household, she does "other things when I know that I have assignments to complete." An executive assistant sees distance learning as providing a "compromise for the ambitious, yet responsible family member" who wants to spend time at home.

> *I do not feel guilty about taking a home study course. It has helped me by giving me more time at home. I no longer spend two hours in traffic. I have meals ready for my children. I can help them study more.*
>
> —Health consultant, 37, married, children at home

A supportive boss

A few women wrote that they don't have to feel guilty about studying at home because they are able to do some course work while on the job.

> *My boss ... allows me time at work to take on my course assignments. At 53 she is also returning to school for her doctorate. The program she is involved in is completely online. We are both homebodies who treasure the time we have at home. ... We take that seriously.*
>
> —Project assistant, distance learning experience

Accreditation

Not all distance education programs are accredited, which means that not all programs have received a comprehensive inspection by reputable accrediting agencies, are declared to have "high standards" (which usually means standards similar to those required of traditional courses and programs), or have a record of delivering what they promise. Bear and Bear (2001) count almost 500 fraudulent college programs—often called degree mills—some of which invent agencies to give accreditation to their schools.

> *In my experience [in a low-income housing project], some people are getting acceptance into bad deals [non-accredited online programs]. Then they take out student loans and they're paying them back and they end up getting nothing for it.*
>
> —Social worker

Many recent studies on the effectiveness of distance learning have asked whether online learning is as effective as traditional learning. But this may be much too limited a focus for an assessment of online learning. Growing numbers of students and programs have increased the demand for high-quality distance learning institutions with clear goals and standards and explicit statements about transferring credits. Attention to gender equity issues (discussed in Part 4 of this report) should be a part of new accreditation standards and practices if federal financial assistance to students or institutions is involved and if these programs are to meet high educational goals for all students and faculty.

Comments

Most women who are going (or, in many cases, returning) to college have multiple responsibilities. Many single parents care for young children, many are the sole provider or co-contributor to their family's income, and some care for aging or ill parents. Some respondents write about their right to continue their education or about the importance to their own careers and to their family income of continuing their education. Others write about the tension between their wish to take courses and their need to fulfill family responsibilities. Most respondents mention income problems. These answers open a window on the ways that women, pulled in these cases by the three shifts of work, family, and school, attempt to reconcile competing demands on their time and energy—often with little institutional, financial, or even emotional support from co-workers, employers, schools, spouses, or children.

The family is, of course, shaped by cultural influences. Women in so-called traditional families constantly allude to their assumptions of their responsibilities to their spouses and children. These mothers feel that their primary responsibility is to meet many of the home, educational, emotional, and medical needs of the others in the home. A few point out that while this is a socially constructed situation, women must deal with the resulting heavy work loads not through social programs that would provide childcare and financial support, but through individual solutions.

Teachers and institutions could help in a number of ways. Recognizing some of the pressures that women, especially, might be experiencing, institutions should consider building more flexibility into their schedules and setting up rent-to-own, leasing, or interest-free loan programs for required equipment. Institutions should interview students who drop out to see if more flexible options would have made a difference in their ability to finish courses.

Part 4

Look Who's Talking:
Gender Identity and Culture Online

 Synchronous or same-time computer-mediated communication differs from asynchronous forms of communication such as e-mail, which do not require that participants be at their computers at the same time. Computer-mediated communication receives a lot of attention from educators and students interested in replacing, perhaps improving on, the kinds of interactions possible in classrooms. Programs such as the Internet Relay Chat enable students and teachers to exchange information in real time. Other text-based programs, such as MUDs (Multi-User Domain) and MOOs (MUD, Object Oriented), allow learners to interact in a virtual world. (In these programs, participants using synchronous discussions create and describe characters, places, objects, and events. MUDs are usually used for role-playing games, while MOOs are usually used for social interaction, including exploration of ideas.) Still other programs allow chats with graphical backgrounds, visible characters associated with each participant, controlled movement of one's character, and other elements intended to make the interaction more interesting and realistic. Ingram, Hathorn, and Evans (2000) discuss some of the opportunities and pitfalls of these programs.

Computer-mediated programs used for social, role-playing, and educational electronic communication will continue to evolve as the use of computer video and audio equipment becomes more functional and widespread. Today educational chat rooms usually show messages in the order participants send them. Students see a list of messages on their screens as messages are posted. When they want to contribute their own messages, they compose their comments on a message window and then send the messages to be included in the electronic discussion. In large classes students often are divided into several smaller groups, which allows for multiple, independent discussions.

Students differ in their interest in participating in online forums, recognizing some of the advantages and drawbacks of the major features of the forums: messages are permanent (they can be read and reread but cannot be undone), messages are public (students can address everyone in the course quickly, which means that there is wide exposure), communication is asynchronous (messages can be written and read when students like, but forums lack visual cues and fluid discussion), and messages can be edited before being sent (students can rewrite to clarify and structure ideas, but composing a text is a discipline) (Hammond, 2000, p. 253). In addition, messages can be written and sent without fear of interruption; therefore, students can claim all the space they want, but their text can be ignored even more easily in an online discussion than can their comments in an oral discussion.

Technology and the Virtual Classroom: The Great Equalizers?

Representing a still common notion about the freedom and equality of online interaction, an Internet expert writes, "One of the best features about life in digital space is that your skin color, race, sex, size, religion or age does not matter; neither [do] academic degrees you have" (Damer, 1998). Others have suggested that when we enter online interaction we can, if we wish, leave behind cultural labels and expectations. Some initially heralded these new forms of communication as open, inclusive, and democratic. The fantasy was that we could readily become who we wanted to be online, regardless of our true backgrounds and experiences, and interact as disembodied equals.

For example, Turkle (1995, p. 178) wrote about how we can each build a new self by cycling through many selves online.

This now appears to be an overly optimistic generalization. We see evidence that, as one critic puts it, "the Internet does not introduce totally new ethnic dynamics, but rather magnifies those that already exist" (Warschauer, 2000, p. 167). Several professors and instructors, for example, describe undergraduate class chat room or discussion list interactions that went astray or got out of hand, resulting in some students dropping out of classes and other students feeling that they were not wanted in class. One professor talked about an "online racial name-calling event that moved from the online discussion space and became a sit-in in front of the administration building."

> *I was advised not to incorporate a chat room in the graduate courses I taught online, as it would be too easy to lose control of the discussion and there would be too much digression.*
>
> —Part-time graduate student, 51

Conversational Styles

In the past two decades, many studies examined patterns of unequal classroom participation between male and female students, yet research on distance learning has rarely explored these themes. This section will review the existing research literature on conversational styles in the online classroom and discussion forum. Contrary to earlier claims that gender, along with race and social class, is invisible in mixed-sex, computer-mediated interaction (Sproull & Kiesler, 1991), recent research indicates that gender asymmetry exists in both synchronous and asynchronous interaction.

Verbosity: who's talking?

In mixed-sex discussion groups, men contribute more turns and more words online than do women (Kramarae & Taylor, 1993; Wolfe, 2000), who are less likely to continue posting when their messages receive no response (Herring, n.d.). When women do persist, their messages receive fewer responses. (For a discussion of these issues, see Herring, n.d.; Herring, Johnson, & DiBenedetto, 1992, 1995; Hert, 1997).

Researchers studying interaction in an online graduate class in the United Kingdom discovered, to their surprise, that far from increasing women's contribution, participation by men increased. Men typically made more—and longer—contributions than women. Women were more likely to be interactive (their messages contained more references to previous contributions). Further, researchers discovered that participants were unaware of gender-typed behavior, having little to say about possible male/female discourse differences until they were shown the analyses of their discussions (Barrett & Lally, 1999).

Most computer-mediated communication studies have not looked at conversational differences between women and men of different ethnic backgrounds, even though previous communication studies indicate, for example, that the conversational factors that silence white women are different from those that silence students of color. Furthermore, the conversational traits of some cultures may conflict with the conversational styles that electronic conversations encourage. For example, Hispanic students are often described as using more physical gestures in their conversations, being reluctant to disagree with others, and being less competitive, so text-based electronic conversations may present a particular barrier for participation by Hispanics.

Joanna Wolfe (2000) studied the interaction of computer-mediated and traditional class discussions in undergraduate English classes. She found that Hispanic women participated more than Hispanic men and white women in the traditional environment; Hispanic women reported disliking computer-mediated conversation and participated less in that environment. White males were most verbal in face-to-face discussions. They decreased their participation in the computer-mediated setting, but they did not report feeling shut out by either of these conversational environments. Asian-American students were the least vocal. Although they increased their participation in the computer-mediated setting, none of the Asian-American students expressed a preference for computer-mediated conversations.

In an interview, a male university professor describes additional differences in technological experience by race/ethnicity and sex:

A lot of women are extremely comfortable with technology. The issues I have to watch out for are more when people are doing face-to-face collaborative group work to make sure that the men don't dominate, because oftentimes that can happen. ... I realize I was immediately just thinking of all the women [who] have been really, really active in my classes or really gotten into the technology, but they were basically all white. Of course [this university] is mostly white. ... If there's [another] dividing line, it's trying to get faculty of color to be involved with thinking about technology, because they tend to have so many other demands on them on campus. For the use of technology, especially among faculty, I don't see a gender line as much as I see a color line.

Specific cultural differences in the communication of various ethnic groups may affect the ways that students participate in course discussion. What is appropriate conversational behavior for some students, including the right amount of talk, may be uncomfortable or inappropriate for others.

Politeness/rudeness

Research by Wolfe (2000) shows that women in computer-mediated discussions are just as likely as men to initiate disagreements, but they tend to use more agreement terms (which can encourage and promote the participation of others) and tend to drop out of conversations rather than continue to defend their ideas when challenged.

A study by Smith, McLaughlin, and Osborne (1997) concludes that women are more likely to thank others, show appreciation, apologize, and be concerned about rudeness. They are more likely to challenge people who seem to be violating rules of politeness.

When I talk with my male colleagues about e-mail messages, I find that they just don't answer a lot of their e-mail messages. For example, some of them say that when they get calls for help—requests for articles or information about their research— from students not in their classes, they just delete those messages. I don't enjoy answering those requests, but I always try to give some help. My husband tells me that when I do that, as a reward I just increase the number of e-mails I get.

—University professor, 50s

Some studies indicate that women participate more actively and with more influence in asynchronous online environments that include a moderator who maintains order and focus (Korenman & Wyatt, 1996). Studies of online classroom interaction have found women participating more (sometimes even more than the male students) when the teacher, regardless of gender, moderates the interaction (Herring, 1999; Herring & Nix, 1997). The presence of an acknowledged leader with the responsibility for ensuring an environment free of incivility or harassment may create a freer atmosphere for women. Although we need further research on online communication patterns, the possibility that women participate more actively in moderated online classrooms has important impli-cations for online education programs. Teachers might think that setting up self-regulating online class discussions is a more democratic policy; however, in effect such a laissez-faire approach allows the most aggressive individuals to dominate the conversation.

Abruptness

Many women worry that their electronic messages might be too abrupt. Research on students' messages from a college-based electronic forum reflects some gender-related differences. Men posted proportionately more messages, and the content of their messages was likely to be more certain and abstract. (For example, a man might reply to a request for advice, "You need a C program. L programs do not work well," while a woman might say, "I had more luck using a C than an L program. Hope this helps. Let me know.") Women's messages were more likely to include polite or soothing words, acknowledge the original sender, and add qualifiers. Further, the women students seemed to prefer learning from other students rather than from more formal channels (Blum, 1999).

This study finds similar concern among some women for tone and style. A divorced graduate student with a child at home recalls "numerous situations with male professors where I've gotten sort of gruff e-mail from them and I think that they are being tough with me but then when I meet with them in person, they're fine and it's not a problem."

> *I respond to dozens of e-mails every day from students, from colleagues who want advice or a citation for an article, from people who need letters of recommendation, and on it goes. I seldom have time to reread the messages I send in reply but when I do I see that I sound too brusque, not pleasant enough. I feel bad about that. But otherwise just answering e-mails would take all day.*
>
> —Professor

Flaming

Anecdotal information on flaming (the sending of contentious, challenging, insulting messages that may demean an interest or concern of an individual or a group of people) has been available for a decade, yet again, there is little formal or systematic research on extreme behaviors online. While some studies (for example, Bell & de La Rue [n.d.]) found that males are more likely to use rude, derogatory language, this subject requires further research.

> *In some electronic communities I am involved in (esp. mailing lists), I've experienced really disgusting behavior by male participants/subscribers. Arrogance, up to hard-core sexism, the whole scale.*
>
> —University professor, 50s

Because of their experience with behaviors online, some women have established women-only online discussion groups (there are relatively few consciously men-only groups). Even when women organize women-only groups, men sometimes ignore the request that they stay out. Researchers have documented a number of cases in which repeated hostile interference by men has forced women-centered online groups to disband, move to another online site, or set up strict rules for online behavior (Collins-Jarvis, 1997; Ebben, 1994; Reid 1994). Since teacher-directed plans for most online classes do not encourage or allow gender-segregated discussion groups, setting clear regulations regarding acceptable participant conduct and monitoring discussions becomes even more important.

Topic control

When using asynchronous communication, many participants can talk at once, without concerns about interrupting or being interrupted. Students no longer have to wait for a teacher to call on them, and students who have trouble articulating their thoughts orally can take their time to think and compose. Hence some researchers and teachers have talked about the advantages of such online discussions for students who are marked by visible cues such as gender, race, and physical disability in traditional courses. However, while such participants *could* write at length without interruption, in actuality women whose comments are not noticed by others often *decrease* their level of participation.

Some research finds that in online discussions, women's topics tend to receive fewer responses from others, both females and males. Women do not usually control the topics of discussion except in groups where women are a clear majority (Herring, n.d.; Hert, 1997).

Silence

What is not said and by whom depends upon not just what kinds of repressive mechanisms are used but also upon cultural ideas of appropriate conversational behavior and upon the coping strategies students use when experiencing sexism and racism. For example, studies of African American adult students indicate that one of the coping responses to obstacles in classes (such as attending discussions that ignore relevant social and cultural experiences) is silence (Johnson-Bailey & Cervero, 1996; Ross-Gordon & Brown-Haywood, 2000).

Students whose native language is not English may have to distort their interests and experiences to participate in online English discussions, where the conversations have an organization, form, and tradition unlike the forms and traditions to which such students are accustomed. For example, members of several Native American tribes (e.g., Apache, Navajo, and Papago) tend to be silent in social situations when the role expectations or the social status of the participants is unclear. Asking them to participate in online conversations with those they do not know or with whom they do not have a defined social relationship may be asking them to commit gross social acts. Also Native American students who must translate from their native languages may have problems expressing themselves quickly in computer-mediated systems (Baldwin, 1995, p. 119). Add to this the social convention of "appropriate silence" (to show respect to elders, for example), and the silence of some Native Americans in online discussions becomes not just something to solve, but something to be understood by other students and teachers.

Some educators extol the relative anonymity of computer-mediated communication networks. The age, social class, ethnicity, and sometimes gender of each of the participants are, at least at times,

unknown by others. Now we also need to pay attention to different cultures and our own assumptions about what an online conversation should look like.

Gender

Prior to this study, many participants had not thought about their experience with gender online. Nonetheless, a substantial number say that they see gender differences in both synchronous and asynchronous interaction.

Haven't thought about this/do not have enough experience to know

Approximately one-third of the women respondents in this study cannot answer the question about whether gender-related differences are present in Internet discussions. Most say they do not yet have any or much experience with web-based discussions or they have not thought about whether such differences exist. Some indicate that they are in predominately female online classes. Many know that women and men interact in somewhat different ways in traditional classes and in other settings, but respondents are not sure what is happening online. A 34-year-old teacher notes that in the traditional classroom "women discuss the hows and whys, men want to know where we are going with this. Online, I don't know."

> *I teach writing classes, and I can see how women enjoy exchanging confidences and finding out personal things about their classmates, such as number of children. Men ask more surface questions such as courses taken. But online—I am not sure, although research says women and men interact in different ways.*
>
> —Professor, 46, married

Computer-mediated communication does not help equalize male/female interactions

Approximately one-fourth of female participants say that computer-mediated communication is not neutral and that women and men interact in different ways in Internet classes. Many argue that men want to connect on a more abstract, solution-based level, while women have more diverse interests (including family, career, philosophy) and want to discuss more and work together. "Women are more prone to handle situations in groups and men want to solve it now. Women discuss a lot more. I've seen men just state opinions, but together both can be very effective," says a self-employed 33-year-old. Others observe the typical differences found in other social settings. As a 22-year-old musician comments, "Men are usually more outspoken, and women speak less [frequently] and more thoughtfully."

> *Most male students are quite skilled at putting up a facade of confidence and self-assurance even if they haven't grasped the content of a lecture. Women tend not to ask questions in mixed-gender groups for fear of appearing stupid, thinking that everyone else (every male?) has understood the subject matter.*
>
> —Research assistant/lecturer, 42, married

A systems analyst provides a detailed analysis of distance learning interaction:

I know that they differ! Being a graduate from a predominantly female college, I found that whenever a man was introduced into the stream of talk, we have them trying to out-speak, out-do or out-talk in order to best the females. Women open topics, not to score but to discover the intricacies of the topic and learn other viewpoints. With a man "that is the way it is" and to challenge him is to insult him, when education should enlighten! Online

the ability to create a pseudo persona is great, but one can find the feminine and masculine traits by the very word choice of the writer and the aggression in their text.

Computer-mediated communication makes discussions more equitable

A smaller number of women see few or no gender-related differences in the ways women and men interact in online courses. These responses emphasize that the lack of visual cues equalizes online students. A 56-year-old program director notes: "Internet discussions seem to put both women and men on an equal level. We cannot see the other person and therefore we are not so conscious of gender." A 40-year-old says online classrooms "level the playing field" because visual cues to identity are not available and "only the personality shows through online."

Other respondents suggest that the equalization of gender relations occurs because of factors inherent in the structure of distance learning. "After all, it really is just typing," notes an itinerant worker. "One has no idea if the 'male' or 'female' is [really of that] specific gender. That is the anonymity of the Internet." Another who attends classes online argues, "Women don't feel the need to defer or be quiet," because only first initials and last names are used for login, and hence gender is masked. These answers assume that gender identity is communicated or revealed primarily through visual presence and is, therefore, not evident in other mannerisms or characteristics online.

Most differences are individual or cultural, not gender-based

A smaller number respond that other factors are more important than gender in determining why people interact as they do online. Some reference age and maturity as more salient features of online discussions and interaction patterns. A high school English teacher says, "It is not so much between men and women as it is between cultures as well as ages." A 28-year-old research associate taking an online course puts more weight on "personality/character over gender."

Other responses

Dozens of the women mention that in online discourse women and men are more open, honest, laid-back, and free. A 27-year-old student writes, "Women feel less apprehensive during Internet discussions." A mental health worker who earned her bachelor's degree through distance learning says, "The Internet provides a certain amount of security since it is not a face-to-face discussion where one can place a face with the opinion." A 40-year-old director of an English language institute states, "Online and in writing, it is easier to be bold and forthright, something difficult for many women to do in person."

> *I have noticed that I react to women and men differently and my Internet discussions have brought this to light. At times when there is no obvious way of knowing whether your cyber-classmate is male or female, or you have discovered that they are the opposite sex of what you guessed, I [think about] my prior conversations with them to ascertain if I have committed any social faux pas.*
>
> —Nurse, 49, single, children at home

Because they do not need to worry about what others might think about them, younger women admit that they change their behavior when taking online courses. A nail technician writes: "No matter what is said, appearances count. If you are at home in your PJs, you're more likely to be paying attention to work rather than to who is paying attention to you."

Student Identity and Gender Dynamics

Distance learning makes access to higher education possible to a great number of previously excluded people. But the increased access involves not just numbers of students, but also diversity in terms of age, ethnicity, gender, class, income, and work and family situations that once limited participation (Herman & Mandell, 1999, p. 17). As a consequence, many other assumptions about higher education (including curriculum) and the process of education must be entertained. Online courses offer special opportunities for working on stereotypes—if institutions support this work.

Social context cues

In face-to-face conversations we make assumptions based on how people appear (including age, skin color, gender, hair styles, clothing, and speech). We guess, for example, about people's intelligence, social status, and ability to do well in university classes. Many of these cues are missing in text-based online discussions. However, what many view as a deficiency of computer-mediated communication, others (including many women in this survey) find a virtue.

Women taking online courses are optimistic about technology as a corrective to subtle—and sometimes not-so-subtle—bias or discrimination in the traditional classroom. More than half the respondents say that online classes without video present less or no possibility of racism, sexism, or homophobia, since students and teachers cannot see or hear each other. Answering a question about whether online classes minimized or eliminated sexism and racism, one respondent illustrates the enthusiasm for online classes as equalizers: "If you never see who you are dealing with, how do you know unless they tell you? Prior to this question, did you know I was African American? Would you have known even with this question if I did not tell you? I think not."

Many people writing about the virtues of the Internet have suggested that its "blindness" reduces racism and sexism and promotes greater freedom of expression and equal exchange among people of different groups. (See, for example, Graham [1999, pp. 141-145].) Online anonymity, a much-touted and in many respects tantalizing feature of the computer culture and the virtual classroom, warrants closer examination: How do missing context cues—facial expressions, sex, skin color, or appearance—change our educational conversations for better or worse?

Gender-bending online?

The possibility that gender online is more malleable than gender in face-to-face interaction has enticed sociologists and observers of life online. With synchronous MOOs, participants can invent new names (nicks) and personalities (characters), hiding their real identities. These gender experiments, however, have received more attention than their relatively small number seems to justify (Headlam, 2000). In a recent study, participants in several social and educational MOOs were asked whether they had ever used a MOO gender other than their biological designation, and, if so, whether they had done so within the last month. Most participants did not gender-switch as part of their online presentation, and, in fact, most of the participants in the social MOOs had never engaged in gender switching. In role-playing MOOs, the majority were either currently switching genders or had switched genders previously (Roberts & Parks, 1999).

In recreational chat rooms, participants often ask the gender of other participants, and they display their own chosen gender through nicknames, message content, and the use of third-person pronouns to describe their actions. One study finds female characters more likely to use affectionate verbs (such as "hugs") and male characters more violent verbs (such as "kills") (Herring, 1998).

While the majority of participants in most chat modes are male, females who participate often receive a lot of attention, much of it sexual in nature (Bruckman, 1993; Herring, 1998, 1999; Rodino, 1997). (In an episode that riveted participants, a character in a social MOO performed a textually enacted rape on a member of their online community. The other characters tried to figure out the relationship of a virtual rape and a physical rape and determine what punishment the attacking character, who operated under a nickname, should receive.) Even among chatters interested in exploring what gender could or should be, many online behaviors are rooted in the old conceptions of gender divisions and hierarchy.

In environments other than games (in education chat rooms, for example), gender is more transparent, because the people enrolled in the courses use their names, which often reveal their gender, and because many view gender-switching as ethically dubious and counter to the expectation that people will be honest.

Even when people play with gender roles, users who present maleness online (whether or not they are male) generally have more power than those who present femaleness (Rodino, 1997). This indicates that while people might briefly change gender online, some of the dominant features remain in action. What would be revolutionary would be new ways for women and men to interact online altogether.

Out of sight, out of mind?

Women and men had a lot to say about whether the new technology used in online courses could help eliminate biases. Since teachers and students cannot see each other, many respondents believe that problems with stereotypes should disappear. For example, a business administration graduate student, 40, taking online courses, states that online (and therefore unseen) students who have experienced discrimination before may have fewer difficulties: "I have had [classroom] experiences where, as an American Indian, I could see others who were non-Indian treated better. I was not given as much time or consideration when I asked questions. ... [In online courses] I can excel in my course work without ... having to compete with the others in my class." A 52-year-old who finished her master's degree online was surprised to discover that her "faculty adviser turned out to be 27 ... while my one study buddy was a great-grandmother. [Initially] I didn't have any idea; I thought we were all about the same age."

> *Online distance education can help eliminate those biases. If all students kept that information to themselves, perhaps then it would eliminate the biases completely (another great social-psychology research question!!).*
>
> —Research associate, 28, single, taking online courses

Old wine, new bottles

Several dozen respondents state that old bases for judgment and bias may be replaced with new cues, especially those of writing style and content:

- A 52-year-old bartender with a learning disability writes, "Things communicated in writing tell much about an individual and a bias can be formed from almost any prejudice."

- A 48-year-old college professor predicts, "Different ways of determining [race, gender, age] may arise; e.g., language use, references, etc. Even if they are wrong, these assumptions will still color people's interactions."

- A 24-year-old graduate student similarly cautions from an instructor's perspective: "In most cases I can tell the gender of a person who wrote an essay because males and females tend to have different perspectives and voices. ... Teachers will in general know what gender they are dealing with, so bias will not be eliminated. Perhaps it will be harder to tell with race and age, but again, there are often tell-tale cultural signs."

- A biology teacher reports: "People were very careful about what they wrote concerning race. Most people identified their age by way of chitchat or by way of relating personal experience. And the male/female status was perhaps the very first thing you established in statements such as 'my husband,' and with names like 'Ann' or 'David,' etc."

> *If a participant is given a number, maybe, but from a linguistic point of view, biases can be detected. You can't wipe out a person's thought processes that include sex/race/age. Go on a chat line and you can clearly see this!*
>
> —Psychologist, 52, single

Others comment that distance learning may create new types of bias around writing or even typing skills. A manager of a technology group responds,

"There is a new bias [involving] technology literacy." A 47-year-old social worker writes that because Native Americans on reservations have less access to technology, they are likely to reveal their inexperience in an online course and may, as a result, experience some discrimination.

> *[Personal] characteristics can be masked via distance learning if students are required to select a name that does not indicate sex, age, etc. I often use "quay" for that reason. It signifies bridge (which ... subconsciously suggests my desire to be accessible and to communicate).*
>
> —Survey design consultant, 55, single

Even more women point out that teachers usually have some personal information about students and always have students' names, which often carry gender and ethnicity information. Respondents suggest that biases could be avoided if numbers were used instead of names and if no personal information were given.

Eliminate bias, not difference

Many responses assume that avoiding any indications or mention of racism and sexism would be the best possible situation in online education. Does this mean that students should be ready to hide their experiences relevant to the course materials and discussions and those that come from their age, ethnicity/race, gender, and sexual orientation? Is this desirable pedagogically?

To the contrary, some educators reject the color-blind or sex-blind ideal and believe that exploration of the connections (gender, age, race, and class) between students and themes of privilege and oppression should be a concern of all education (see, for example, Tisdell [1998]).

While most women in this survey applaud the success or potential success of distance learning in minimizing negative biases, many do not necessarily believe that online courses can mask differences among students, nor do they endorse this as a desirable goal. Respondents value explicit identification of differences in online discussions and courses for a variety of reasons. Some feel that avoidance of differences and potential bias will not make the problem go away. Similarly, a few respondents write that it is a valuable part of the educational process for students to confront their own assumptions about others and to challenge others' biases. "Online education just masks reality and minority students' opportunities to take on prejudice head-on," writes a 24-year-old doctoral candidate. A male data entry contractor notes, as well, that distance education "could have the unintended effect of preserving people's biases by protecting them from personal experience with people who disprove their stereotypes."

> *Yes, [distance education] could help weed out sex/race/age biases on the part of the teacher and other students. But I also think that some learning is lost in the process. I guess I would rather put more money into classes in middle schools and high schools in the spirit of preventive medicine than shield sex/race/age biases from happening to women later on.*
>
> —Family transportation specialist

Others underscore that anonymity or disguised identities threaten to "take away ... the essence of a person," as a 42-year-old professor describes. A flight attendant agrees: "I do not like to see gender removed. Women and men have different perspectives that are very valuable to teach different segments of society."

> *If we want to eliminate [students' personal characteristics], we'd have to become really impersonal. ... As courses become more impersonal and remote from human interaction and knowing who we are, it would be more difficult for [them] to succeed.*
>
> —Technology coordinator, 45, married, two children at home, distance learning experience

Face-to-Face Contact

Face-to-face contact in the classroom has many functions. For example, many teachers rely on eye contact as affirmation that a student is paying attention (although in some cultures it would be viewed as staring and a cultural taboo [Spring, 1995]), and students may signal their lack of interest in or understanding of material by avoiding eye contact or sleeping.

When asked whether seeing the reactions of others in a classroom is important, most U.S. teachers reply that it is very important. Several add that while it is vital to them as teachers, it is less important to them when they are students themselves. A former computer science teacher comments: "As a teacher it is through eye contact, especially with women, that I get the feeling if the class understands the lecture or if they are totally confused. However ... as a student it is not really that important to me. ... In a pure lecture environment, it is distracting to have others physically in the same room. [And] if you make your opinions known and someone bristles, then you fear the hostility in the classroom, where it should be freedom of expression."

However, most student respondents indicate that making contact and seeing the reactions of others, especially of teachers, are very important or at least important in some situations.

Contact is important
Nearly one-third of respondents find face-to-face contact important for a variety of reasons. They

include camaraderie ("Life and learning is a social event," explains a 40-year-old outdoor guide, and another respondent wants more than "book sense" out of her education), the motivation that can come from hearing the experiences of others, increased professional contacts, and social interaction with other adults (the latter may be especially important for single parents). Others cite the stimulation that can result from friction and disagreement in the classroom and the problems they have faced trying to deal with disagreement online. A graduate student finds: "Not having eye contact can lead to misunderstandings. I've had my share of cyber fights with people because of misinterpreting something. And once the words are written, you can't go back and erase them, versus when you are in person when someone says something, you can explain it away a little easier."

Other women note the value of hearing sarcasm, jokes, and subtleties of tone. "Looking at others is particularly important for women," says a computer programmer. "If I get upset in a conversation I just look at the person I like and ignore the others. ... There is something visceral about the importance of attention in the classroom." Some stress that students express themselves and learn in ways other than through words. Many state that interaction with others is the primary way they learn—that teaching and learning are relational processes best achieved in face-to-face settings.

> *I still want to see somebody. I haven't turned into an online shopper, because I still want to touch and feel whatever I'm buying. ... But I guess I'm sort of old school.*
>
> —Video producer, 29

No, getting the course credit is more important

Dozens of women respond negatively when asked if seeing the reactions of others in a classroom is important to them. Many women reply that what is most important right now is the degree itself, however it can be obtained. A few women cite logistical problems and subordinate issues of contact or social interaction to convenience. "I don't feel I have the option," comments a marketing consultant. "Online, I can finish my senior year no matter where my husband's job takes us." These answers imply that women may view contact as a social or expendable component of the educational experience. As a 25-year-old registered nurse explains, "Contact and reactions is not my priority ... I am all about learning and progressing to another level."

Several draw an age distinction and say that physical interaction is no longer their priority. A 31-year-old seamstress says contact is less important than it used to be: "With the social element ... eliminated, it is all about the learning for me now. I have friends and a full life. I am looking to expand my knowledge base for both financial gains and personal growth." An instructor of biology similarly notes that face-to-face contact matters less at this point than it did during his earlier college years.

Having contact with others is important in some situations

For many respondents, seeing and reacting with others is valuable, but only part of the time. Contact is "an extra bonus ... but not a needed requirement," a 46-year-old computer system support analyst states. Many say that being able to see others is not essential for a rewarding educational experience, but it is an added perk. "Sometimes it is nice to know if I'm not the only one not getting it," a 24-year-old layout engineer comments.

Some students in online courses think that making contact with other students is more important for some courses than others. Contact is deemed important for people-oriented courses and visual courses such as psychology and art but not so important for math and science courses.

Contact is particularly valuable at the beginning of a course

Online graduate students who are required to spend some time together on campus believe the experience is critical to the success of subsequent online discussions. One Latina, who writes that her online classmates are a very diverse and mature group including white, Latina, and black women, a Lebanese woman, and two men in their late 30s, says: "The time we spent together was like 'boot camp' because if we weren't in class we were studying [together]. ... During class a lot of issues came out (race, gender, etc.) and we discussed our individual viewpoints; it was a little messy in the beginning, but ... we accepted each other's viewpoints and now we can discuss online more freely."

Technology *does* allow for contact

Several dozen women argue that contact is important and that distance learning classes accomplish this goal. They point out that they can still get reactions through writing and chat room conversations rather than through primarily visual cues. A 33-year-old single mother writes, "When I was online I made 'the speaker' aware I was listening by adding my opinions when asked." Some women clarify that contact online is just as meaningful as face-to-face but may require the development of new social competencies and skills. An academic adviser explains, "Contact can be simulated in a distance learning environment, it just takes a little more effort." A flight instructor notes the importance of experience, "Once you are online and actively participating in discussions, you learn the reactions and make contacts just as easily as face-to-face."

Others add that new and future technology will allow for greater visual and even tactile learning online. "Facial expressions are an important part of some interactions," comments a single mother returning to school online, "so a camera onsite and at home would fix that, but there's a lot to be said about the safety of anonymity."

> *Visual/tactile learning is important, especially with challenged learners; however, with today's technology, we have 2D visuals, sound, and graphics. [On the other hand,] I cannot [understand chemistry experiments] without feeling, seeing or smelling the reactions in some way.*
>
> —Help desk/systems analyst, children at home

Some respondents note that an online global student body can provide diversity and a cultural richness that is otherwise nearly impossible to represent in a traditional course. They note that this is only true, however, if student expertise and understandings are considered a part of the course material. Now studying in the United States, a young Fulbright scholar from Russia suggests that effective global education "can only come from knowing about other cultures." She recommends that teachers from several countries jointly develop courses and points out that foreign students studying in the United States often find that professors "ignore what isn't immediate to them."

Learning is easier when we are by ourselves

Several dozen women give primacy to the importance of *not* having face-to-face contact. Most of them focus on the pleasure of being able to spend more time thinking about possible answers and the best ways of phrasing them. Others indicate that unless they know classmates well, they are unlikely to read reactions accurately in any case. A 19-year-old au pair argues, "People can become either inhibited or encouraged [by others' nonverbal reactions], depending on how they perceive themselves in relation to other students. For example, if you believe that you are not as competent and knowledgeable, you're most likely to side with the [dominant] discussion and not express your opinions. In an online setting, people generally feel freed of such pressures."

More than a dozen women value privacy and the chance to work alone more than interaction with students. A paralegal explains, "I like working alone or with a small group of people I trust, like, and respect. You can't always find that in a classroom."

Comments

Given their choice, most students and teachers would prefer to have face-to-face contact in their courses. At present most online courses do not provide a good video approximation of what people can see in a classroom. Students who *need* online courses are willing to forego the advantages of face-to-face interaction for the greater advantage of being able to complete their courses and programs. Some point out that we can learn to read reactions of others more accurately through their written responses. A favored solution to some of the problems of online learning is to have some face-to-face sessions during a course.

Online Isolation: Lonely or Alone Online?

Popular wisdom holds that women value interactive experiences in education, personal relationships with advisers and counselors, and collaborative learning. With these assumptions in mind, does online learning make women feel *less* connected to students or lonelier in their education? Some of the major primary considerations are listed below from most frequent responses to least. Many replies reject a strict division between being connected and being lonely.

Most women who have experience with online education are more positive about the social and educational possibilities of web-based education than those who do not have that experience, which indicates that perhaps women have preconceived ideas that online learning will be more isolating than those who pursue it actually experience it to be.

I am as connected as most on-campus students are, but in different ways

Most respondents who had experienced some online learning write about ways that they feel *more* connected online than they did in on-campus courses. Many write that initially they felt isolated (one woman writes that she felt as if she were functioning in a sensory deprivation tank), especially since they had always gauged the impact of their words by watching facial and physical reactions. They learned new ways of making connections, however, and discovered that while online they were "only an e-mail away" from teachers, advisers, and other students. Some women feel *more* connected to their advisers and teachers because of the possible immediacy of e-mail.

Many women emphasize that a distance learning student can, in one woman's terms, be "as connected as [she] want[s] to be, and after log-off,

we can each focus on our families or partners for social needs." Others distinguish between being lonely and alone. "I wouldn't say I was lonely, more like alone," a paralegal clarifies. "I feel connected enough that when I need my mentors, I can reach them." Similarly, a retired student describes distance learning as independent rather than lonely and "connected to information but not to other people."

Course structure and student preferences in large measure determine the ease and level of interaction among students. In this respect online courses resemble any traditional classroom course. Notes a housing developer: "In a previous online course, I didn't like it because of the non-interaction. My current class is completely different. We have e-mail discussions and mandatory online chat room weekly. We can also set up a chat without the instructor being present. ... All these factors provide a feeling of classroom without the faces."

Other students focus on the adjustments teachers and students make to facilitate online connections. "I have to dazzle others with my writing skills as opposed to my dynamic personality," explains a 30-year-old teacher. Another teacher states: "I feel connected, but I chose my words wisely since you can't see my smile. I am wordy, mainly because I don't want to come across as cross or short with anyone; that is very important to me since most classmates have never met me face-to-face. I write in a lot of lowercase letters so I don't come across as haughty and I use ... [ellipses] to show natural pauses I would take if I talked with people."

> *I learned to be more precise in my delivery, to use humor a lot less or explain my humor a lot more. Now I would say I feel like a viable member of my classes.*
>
> —Psychologist, 41, married, children at home, distance learning experience

Who needs more social life!

Teachers, more than online students, stress the importance of learning as a social activity. For example, a 65-year-old university teacher argues that she has to "see and hear my students. The stimulation you get from other students, and from the environment, and from the teacher—I think it's healthy." As adults with jobs or careers or families, however, most student respondents do not feel as impassioned about the traditional collegiate culture. They have a firm allegiance to their roles as students but also to their roles as workers, parents, partners, or spouses. In this they are similar to on-campus adult undergraduate students. (Donaldson, et al., 2000, p. 8).

> *Social aspect of distance learning? Who cares? There is a bar on the corner.*
>
> —Industrial technical educator, 32, single

Age emerges once again as a critical issue, with older students likely to minimize the importance of social experiences or interaction in the classroom, which, in one woman's terms, are "traditionally more important to the younger student." "I am an older student," a 30-year-old single mother explains. "Younger students will benefit more from the traditional mode of educational pursuits and their funders (parents) would surely prefer them to be on campus where they are more secure and supervised. However, it is the nontraditional audience that distance education will cater to and benefit." Indeed, a 40-year-old professor predicts that online classes could "connect better than even traditional, especially for older students. What I like is the possibility of working with others who have rich experience that you may not get in a regional traditional college. However, if there is no chance for online discussion ... it can be very lonely (just like a traditional class)."

Other women experience traditional classes as lonely and isolating, especially if they commute to campus. "I was not able to connect with other students because of the commute," a doctoral candidate recalls. "Working during the day did not allow me to take off to ... meet with peers. ... I think it would be great for once if the class could come to me whether in the office or at home." Others answer the question about whether online education might be isolating by pointing out that they feel less intimidated talking online than they do talking in the classroom. One 31-year-old student and substitute teacher says that in her traditional classes, most students rarely talk to each other, unless they know each other outside class. In her online class, in which there is less social anxiety, students get to know each other much better.

Distance learning is isolating

The third most frequent response is that women feel isolated in online classes and miss the personal interaction of a classroom. As an accountant explains, "I also know that my instructor knows nothing about me except for the few bits of information I gave at the introductory section of the course." Others complain about a lack of body language to help interpret what is being said.

A university instructor (and author of a book based primarily on responses of on-campus returning women) thinks that women should not so readily accept their designation as prime candidates for distance education. She stresses what she thought of as especially important for women who are single parents:

> The last thing that single moms need is continued distance from the campus. Women should not be bullied into believing that distance learning is the same as a campus education. Women in distance learning are isolated. Women should not be "siphoned off" into distance learning, which doesn't have the same prestige as regular campus degrees, anyway. Women taking distance learning courses are very credit-hour focused, very family-oriented. Education is on the margin. They are eating the chicken wing ... taking what's left over. Many often actually have more options. ... Women should have information about the free tuition available to seniors at some state colleges and universities, and other funding available for single moms returning to university.

Loneliness depends upon the needs of the student

Some students report that they "work best without distractions, and other students are sometimes a distraction," in the words of a bartender. Alternately, they speculate that a social person may feel cheated online. As a manager states, "If a person is apt to make friends, they are apt to do so [despite] the circumstances."

Persons in a wheelchair are most often persona non grata. They are mostly considered in the way. So distance education would not bother me at all.

—Unemployed, 51, married, uses a wheelchair

Online is best when combined with on-campus interaction

Many programs require periodic on-campus attendance, and some respondents think on-campus attendance should be required for distance learning courses. They favor a hybrid approach that includes "time at intervals to meet with faculty and fellow students," as a social worker describes.

It can get tiresome to be on the PC for too long. The social aspect is needed for a complete learning experience. Although sometimes I can interact with others via e-mail to share and confirm what I believe, I still seek a warm body to sit and have conversations with about [my classes]. As a woman in the field of computer technology, I find it even more important to do this.

—Computer system support analyst, 46, married, children at home

Other perspectives

A few women believe that as more people become comfortable with the changing computer-based ways of communication, more students will feel positive about online education. This study indicates that this is already happening, and those who have considerable computer or online experience are more positive about the possibilities of online education.

Part 5

Conclusions and Recommendations

 In the past, distance learning courses in the United States have been closely associated with off-campus women and "practical needs" courses—courses isolated from regular higher education and removed from academic excellence. Today university administrators and education businesses are becoming increasingly interested in ways of using new information technologies to promote and integrate online learning as part of their traditional programs and, in some cases, as for-profit parallel programs.

Who will produce and deliver the learning materials? Who will decide what kinds of programs are offered and the content of courses? What efforts will be made, and by whom, to ensure that uses made of the new technologies do not reinforce social disparity and limited theories of pedagogy?

The following recommendations will help ensure positive changes.

Recommendations for College/University Policy

- **Treat distance learning students as responsible and intelligent beings, not as passive educational consumers.** This should be a guiding principle for all planning and policy.

- **Recognize that older students using distance education are a less homogenous group than on-campus students.** A major difficulty in planning for older students' educational concerns is the lack of information about their situations and strategies. This report describes some of these differences.

- **Involve women administrators, students, and teachers as active participants and advisers in the planning process for online courses.** Given the heavy participation of women in distance

learning courses and programs, they, especially, should be encouraged to evaluate their situations and needs and make recommendations. In the past they have been the primary, albeit invisible, receivers of distance learning; in the future they could serve as primary evaluators and planners of online courses and programs.

- **Make explicit the institution's mission statements regarding distance-learning plans.** What are the goals? To allow students to increase their ability to understand their place in their society? To serve a greater number of students in the region? To increase students' ability to find employment? To secure a place in the distance learning market? To increase institutional profits? To try to recoup the (often heavy) expenses of distance education? All these and more? Making clear the relationship of the various goals of the institution will help everyone involved— administrators, staff, teachers, and students.

> *Most universities don't really feel that they're accountable to their customers/ students for the product delivered. They think they're accountable to lots of other constituencies—professors, parents, alums, boards of directors, donors.*
>
> —Administrator/professor/director of a communications program, 47

- **Find suitable mechanisms for the continual evaluation of online programs,** including student and teacher involvement.

- **Establish places for online students to talk face to face, when possible.** A technology consultant for a low-income housing project cautions that even if it were possible to put a computer into every apartment, it is also important to have a computer lab in the building —a place for people to congregate in person, discuss course work, learn together, and get technological support if needed.

- **Find ways to make older women students feel welcome online.** Well-planned online programs already include learner support services such as counseling. However, even students who are no older than the average university student but who have children or are working full time feel that they are too old to return to classes. Many women who do not have institutional support for their continuing education worry about whether they will be successful in their return to higher education classes. Attention to their concerns will raise their enrollment and success rate. Some programs have special buddy systems, with successful older students acting as guides and mentors for the incoming students.

- **Combine efforts across programs, colleges, and universities to make political leaders and policy-makers aware of problems (including financial) that adult women, especially, face when trying to continue their formal education**. Bring pressure on government to ensure that students admitted to accredited online programs can receive scholarships and loans.

- **Broadly disseminate information on scholarships and loans for online programs**. Many of the students most interested in online courses suffer from limited funds, and many do not have life styles that bring them in contact with standard bulletin boards and educational journals that ordinarily post information about funding. In some cases, traditional grants and loans do not cover the costs of online education.

- **Explore and publicize the hidden costs of not investing in women's online education.** Adult women's education has not been a major political priority, although women's participation in the workplace has been recognized as critical for the national good.

- **Provide teachers of distance learning courses with consolidated material, such as contained in this report, on the many social and equality issues involved with distance learning.** Research based on conventional classroom arrangements may not translate to the online learning context.

- **Interview students who drop out,** to see if more flexible options would have helped them complete courses.

- **Consider rent-to-own leasing or interest-free loan programs for required equipment.**

Recommendations for Presentation of Course Materials Online

- **Ensure that promotional materials for online education, as well as courses themselves, provide information and guidance relevant to women and other underrepresented groups.**

- **Develop policies for respecting others and codes of conduct online, and make them available as part of the course materials.**

- **Encourage teachers to become informed about computer-mediated communication research and serve as moderators of online class discussions.** A laissez-faire approach allows the most aggressive individuals to have the most freedom. While single-sex groups might not be feasible or even permitted in many online courses, the knowledge that women in single-sex groups are more supportive of each other and more understanding of the kinds of difficulties many women experience when they have young families may help teachers and students find ways to encourage supportive behavior, even in mixed-sex groups.

Recommendations for Teachers and Instructors

- **Clarify for everyone—administrators, students, and teachers—the learning needs that are addressed by the new technology in each program.** Tell students why specific methods (such as requiring participation in chat rooms) are being used. An administrator of one distance teaching university states that tension exists over which takes priority: the technology or the learning needs of students.

- **Recognize different learning methods, and diversify approaches and methodologies used in online education.** Students have distinctive learning systems based on cultural learning processes.

- **Make positive pluralism one of the goals of all online programs.** Create opportunities for every student to participate as fully as possible in online classroom discussions.

Recommendations for Government and National Policies

- **Provide loans for students currently unable to qualify because they are taking low course loads.**

- **Consider what groups of potential online students are likely to be ignored by online programs.** Children of migrant workers are entitled to access to education and training and may benefit from online courses. Online courses could be a great resource for individuals who have to move for political or economic reasons or for prison inmates who have legal rights to the public educational system. Policy-makers must take into account the wide variety of social contexts and needs of online students. One course does not fit all, contrary to recent discussions about the possibility of a set lesson plan cheaply distributed to many.

Recommendations for Research

Universities can play a large role in establishing new research programs to examine small- and large-scale social applications of online learning and culture. This is critical if universities are going to continue to be a base for research and educational policies. Otherwise, industry is likely to fill this role—and industry's questions and concerns often are different from those of people concerned about social equality and intellectual vigor. A caveat, however, is that researchers in colleges and universities are notoriously ready to study and critique institutions and behaviors other than their own. In this time of rapid changes in higher education, everyone will benefit from reflective, open evaluations of online courses and programs.

The following research questions could provide important analyses of online education policy and practice.

Online conversation

- Can gender differences in computer-mediated conversations in online courses be generalized across computer program formats, assignments, and course topics?

- Does participation in online discussion change depending upon whether the teacher is female or male and depending upon the ratio of women and men in the class? This study reports that online conversations are often not equitable. For teachers and students to know how to best prepare for, organize, and participate equitably online, more research on the specifics of conversations and satisfaction levels is needed.

Structure of distance learning programs

- How can distance learning work best for women (and men) with family and career responsibilities and plans? If we want distance learning to work for people with many time demands and other pressures, we will sponsor more research about how women and men actually try to fulfill their (often competing) family wishes and their career wishes and how distance learning can be best structured to work with their goals, rather than simply assume that distance learning (in whatever form) is a good (or the only) option for women with children.

- What pedagogical and economic goals of teachers, students, administrators, and investors can the broad application of the new technologies help achieve?

- Why are many potential learners not participating in distance learning courses? What valuable information can be gathered from students who do not finish online courses and programs?

Access to distance learning courses
- What access do students have to computers?

- What kind of equipment is available at home and at work, and when can it be used for online courses?

- How are computer time and work space allocated within households?

Appendices

Methodology

 Many traditional research methods were not appropriate for this study.
First, the process under consideration —online education—is changing so rapidly that focusing on the description and statistics of any one moment or month or year would make the study a historical rather than an analytical contribution to a volatile issue. Second, since the people potentially involved in online education include most literate adults in the United States, any random sample would require a very large number of respondents; otherwise, little could be reliably concluded about women or men of any age, race, ethnic group, geographical location, education level, or occupation. Higher education students are becoming less uniform; therefore, listening as people describe their needs, educational goals, and experiences is becoming more important.

We decided to gather as many viewpoints as possible through structured but flexible interviews and open-ended questionnaires. While news reports have provided information about the online education plans of many businesses and some online administrators, we knew little about the concerns and plans of present and potential students and teachers. We interviewed women and men of many ages, occupations, and economic levels; some respondents were taking online courses and some were not. College and university administrators, librarians, teachers, business executives, and computer specialists were also interviewed.

We conducted a series of pilot interviews to test the questions the interviewers planned to use. We then revised the questions using insights from related studies. Since little research exists about women and online higher education in the United States, we emphasized qualitative rather than quantitative methods.

Tools

Focus groups
Interviewers met with six focus groups, which were homogenous by occupation. The focus groups included a total of 27 people.

Individual in-depth interviews
We interviewed 64 women and 36 men, including students, administrators, teachers, potential students, former students, business executives, and online education researchers. Ninety-six interviewees live in the United States. Fourteen interviews were conducted by telephone.

The interviews were conducted by the author (a white female professor with more than two dozen years of researching and teaching about technology and gender issues) or a graduate student who was an AAUW intern (either a white man who has done research on society and new technologies or a woman of color—a university staff member—who interviewed people in her community and place of employment). The interviews ranged from twenty minutes to more than two hours and were conducted in classrooms, homes, offices, coffee shops—wherever the person or the situation suggested.

Almost everyone asked to participate in a face-to-face interview agreed. Interviewees were not offered a cash award for their participation. Many knew about previous AAUW research and quickly indicated their willingness to talk about this topic.

Interviewees came from diverse social classes, race and ethnic groups, age groups, and occupations. We used a questionnaire; however, during each interview, we further developed questions in step with the interests and concerns of the interviewees.

We transcribed all interviews, with some transcripts running more than 30 pages.

Online survey questionnaires

Respondents completed 410 online questionnaires between June 2000 and February 2001, and interviewers followed up by e-mail or telephone. Respondents, who found the survey through Internet-based networks, Internet searches, or the AAUW website, included 398 women (350 from the United States) and 12 men (10 from the United States). Clients at an agency helping low-income women were told about the site and encouraged to complete the questionnaire.

Respondents all had some access to the Internet through computers at home, work, libraries, or the homes of friends and relatives. Many were engaged in a course of study or research or were interested in returning to college or university. Participants in the online survey were eligible for a drawing of a $100 honorarium.

All respondents supplied information about their occupations. Almost all the respondents supplied names, e-mail addresses, and mailing addresses, as well as information regarding age, marital status, and number of children at home. Almost all who were asked follow-up questions were willing to cooperate further, and in some cases respondents continued to send e-mail messages for months.

Mann and Stewart (2000) outlined the advantages of online questionnaires (including the possibility of more leisured, considered responses to questions) and the disadvantages (including the possibility that respondents may more readily decline to answer some of the questions or quit halfway through). In this study, most of the respondents answered all or nearly all of the questions.

Additional sources of information

The researchers also used the following information:

- Notes taken in classrooms and in homes where people were working on courses online

- Notes from classrooms where teachers and students were giving presentations about their online work

- Notes from conferences where company representatives were exhibiting software programs and educators were giving presentations

- Notes from discussions with academic colleagues about the theoretical, pedagogical, and social underpinnings of the debates about distance education

- Relevant materials (including surveys) from university administrators, business people, educational foundations, research libraries, and the Internet

About the Respondents

Respondents supplied the brief descriptions following the feature quotes in this report. Initially we collected information on class status, but most people found that designation difficult (often describing several changes in their class status during their lives), so the class description is not included. Descriptions of race/ethnicity were gathered in the interviews but are used here only when the respondents themselves call attention to it. In general, those in the majority group (white) spoke of their race/ethnicity only when prompted.

Respondents listed a wide variety of occupations and fields including, for example, academia (student, vice president of distance learning, dean of education, alumni director), health (herbalist, psychologist, medical receptionist), military (soldier, Army intelligence officer), business (financial consultant, mortgage banker), technology (webmaster, programmer, hardware company executive), publishing (writer, editor), law (attorney, legal assistant, police officer), politics (retired state legislator), religion (parish priest), music (trumpet player), and services (baby-sitter, bartender, flight attendant).

Questions Asked

Interviews and questionnaires dealt with the following general areas: Who is using the new media and under what conditions? What do people see as potential inequalities? What do they see as factors that will affect their opportunities to use the new technologies for their educational interests?

The questions and responses fell into five major categories: aspirations and needs; ideas about the future of higher education; experiences, worries, and successes; access; and connections and caring.

In-depth interview questions

In-depth questions were designed to encourage participants to reflect upon their educational experiences and expectations, focusing particularly on the possibilities and problems of online education. We wanted to capture concerns and interests that may have been ignored in surveys about technology and education, especially women's concerns and interests. See the protocol on page 66.

Online survey questions

Recognizing that people who use computers and are interested in obtaining a higher education degree or in returning to course work might have particularly relevant ideas about online education, we posted an online questionnaire. (Lee [2000, p. 118] and other researchers suggest that investigating the uses of the Internet might be an especially appropriate way of using the Internet as an information resource.) Computer users were asked about their involvement and interest in higher education, both online and on campus. The first 10 respondents were asked how long they spent answering the questions; their responses ranged from 15 to 40 minutes. The online questionnaire, with questions based on the stories and insights gleaned in the interviews and other research documents, is included on page 67.

Face-to-Face Interview Protocol

Name   City
Occupation   Full or part time
Age   Sex   Race
Class/socioeconomic group   In childhood   Now
How did you finance/are you financing education?
What post-secondary education have you received?
Married or with a partner   Children

1. Aspirations, needs
   What are your educational goals?
   What kinds of learning do you need for what you want to do in the
      next five years?
         For vocation or career purposes?
         Academic purposes?
         Personal knowledge and pleasure?
   What do you anticipate needing later in life?
   When you make decisions about your life, do you have to consider
      a spouse or partner and family matters?

2. Ideas about the future of higher education
   What technological changes do you anticipate in higher education
      instruction that will affect your plans?
   Think of your ideal education process.
      What are the elements?
      What does it look like?
      How does it work?
   How do you think you'd like to use the new technologies to make
      things work better for you?
   If you were designing the courses and the technology, what would
      you want them to do? How would you want them to work?
   Did you enjoy being on campus? Would you want to return?

3. Experiences, worries, successes
   What have been your best education experiences?
   Describe the best teacher you ever had. What made her or him
      the best?
   Describe your worst teacher. What happened? What would you
      have done to correct this if you could?
   What kinds of classes have you liked the best?
   How do you most enjoy learning?
   What would you change to make college/adult education courses
      work better for you?
   If you have used DL
      Was taking a DL course your first choice (over taking a course
         in a traditional classroom)?
      Has taking a DL course allowed you to do something you
         wouldn't have been able to do otherwise? If so, what?
      What was the best class you ever had in DL? Worst? Why?
      How did you receive materials and instruction? Voice mail, video-
         conference, web courses, e-mail, audio conference? Other?
      Which was highly effective? Which not?
      What did you expect the experience to be? Did you have any
         expectations, fears, anxieties, or excitement going in?
         If so, what were they?
      How did your experience differ from your expectations?
      Did you have any or much interaction with teachers and
         other students?
      Do you think DL is an improvement or a liability over
         traditional classrooms?
      Can you share a story about your dealings with DL when things

worked? When things didn't work?
      Do you say, write, think or do things in the DL environments
         that you wouldn't do in a classroom?
      Is it easier or harder in a DL course to feel that you've
         communicated your points?
      Does DL make the juggling of multiple responsibilities (work,
         family, etc.) easier or more difficult?

4. Access
   What information technologies (telephone, cell phone, answering
      machine, TV, satellite, cable, VCR, CD player, personal
      computer, laptop, e-mail programs, Internet access) do you
      have? At home? At work? For which of these have you made
      the purchase?
   What technologies do you most want?
   If you were creating the technologies, what would you create to
      make your life better?
   What time restrictions do you have?
      If married or living with a partner, do you have more restrictions
         than they have?
   When taking classes, how do you handle demands on your
      time from family, job, other?
   Who has first computer rights at home?
   What kind of technical training/interest/resources do you have?
   When you need technical help to whom do you go?
      Do you get help?
   Are you able to use a car for study-related purposes (such as driving
      to a study center)?
   What are your financial constraints? Do you consider costs when
      deciding what courses to take and when and where to take them?

5. Connections, caring
   Do you enjoy studying with others? What, if anything, do you value
      about face-to-face meetings in class?
   What do you miss about the traditional classroom, if anything?
      What would you miss about the DL experience if you were in
         a traditional classroom?
   Do you enjoy classroom discussions? Participate in them?
   Would you be more or less likely to participate in discussions held
      via computers? How about interactional video hookups?
   Is it important to feel that you are connected to the teacher and/or
      other students? If so, what kinds of connections make you most
      satisfied with your course experience?
   To whom would you recommend distance learning?
      What kind of person or student?
      Why?
      Who would dislike it?
   Do you think that women and men have (or will have) similar
      experiences in DL classes?
   What has been the gender composition of the courses you've taken,
      either traditional or DL?
   In your classroom experience (traditional or online), who contributes
      the most—women or men?
   Does the type of classroom (traditional and DL) change the power
      dynamics in any way?
   What makes you participate more often? What makes you
      participate less often?
   When you feel uncomfortable participating much, what is the
      environment like? What makes you uncomfortable?
   What kind of instructor helps you participate?

Online Survey Questionnaire

Male or Female
Occupation?
Age
Single __ Married __ Other ___
Number of children under 18 living at home

When was the last time you took a course for credit or toward a degree?

Do you have your own computer at home or access to someone else's computer at home? In what rooms?

Do you have access to a home computer whenever you want to use it?

Do you have access to a computer at work that you could use for distance education purposes? Please explain.

Please briefly describe one of your best educational experiences (regardless of whether any special technologies were involved).

Please briefly describe one of your worst educational experiences (regardless of whether any special technologies were involved).

Could you take a distance education course if you decided to, without consultation with other family members? Is time, or cost, an important consideration? Please explain.

Would you prefer a traditional instructional delivery method or distance education if you had a choice? Please explain.

Do you think that distance education is a good alternative to classroom study when it is the only way to take a course? Please explain.

How do you feel about the social aspect of distance education? Connected? Lonely? Please explain.

Do you feel that you have enough technical support to take a distance education course? Would concerns about technological support prevent you from taking distance education courses? Please explain.

Do you think that women and men interact in different ways from each other in traditional classrooms? Please explain.

Do you think that women and men interact in different ways from each other in Internet discussions? Please explain.

Is making contact and seeing the reactions of others in a classroom important to you? Please explain.

Would you feel guilty taking distance education courses at home when there was other work at home to do? Is your time at home basically yours to decide how to use? Please explain.

Do you plan to use distance education courses in the future to obtain a degree? For personal knowledge and pleasure? For career advancement? Please explain.

Do you learn primarily through discussions, through independent work, or through group work? Please explain.

Do you think that distance education can weed out sex/race/age biases on the part of the teacher and other students? Please explain.

What kind of student do you think is most suited to taking distance education courses?

About the Researcher

Cheris Kramarae is the author, editor, or co-editor of more than 70 articles and 10 books on gender, language, technology, and education. Her edited books include *For Alma Mater: Theory and Practice in Feminist Scholarship* (with Paula Treichler and Beth Stafford); *Knowledge Explosion: Generations of Feminist Scholarship* (with Dale Spender); *Women, Information Technology, and Scholarship* (with H. Jeane Taylor and Maureen Ebben); and *Technology and Women's Voices*. Her most recent publication is the four-volume *Routledge International Encyclopedia of Women: Global Women's Issues and Knowledge* (co-edited with Dale Spender).

Former director of women's studies at the University of Illinois at Urbana-Champaign, Kramarae has taught in universities in a number of countries, including China, the Netherlands, England, and South Africa. In 1999-2000 she was an international dean at the International Women's University (Internationale Frauenuniversität) in Germany as well as project director for the courses "The Future of Education," and "The Construction of Gender on the Internet" during the 2000 session. She is now a visiting researcher at the Center for the Study of Women in Society at the University of Oregon.

Kramarae's teaching has included hybrid university courses, which combine face-to-face and online interaction. She was a co-organizer of the WITS (Women, Information Technology, and Scholarship) work and study group and participated in the early stages of task force innovations in the use of computer technology in university courses at the University of Illinois at Urbana-Champaign.

Bibliography

Bibliography

Agustín, Laura. (1999). They speak, but who listens? In Wendy Harcourt (Ed.), *Women@Internet: Creating new cultures in cyberspace* (pp.149-161). London: ZedBooks.

Albrecht, Gary L. (1992). *The disability business: Rehabilitation in America.* Newbury Park, CA: Sage.

American Association of University Women Educational Foundation. (1999). *Gaining a foothold: Women's transitions through work and college.* Washington, DC: Author.

American Federation of Teachers. (2000, August 18). *E-testimony to the Web-Based Education Commission.* Retrieved June 27, 2001, from http://www .webcommission.org/directory

American Library Association, Presidential Committee on Information Literacy. (1989). *Final report.* Chicago: Author. Retrieved June 27, 2001, from http://www.ala .org/acrl/nili/ilit1st.html

American Library Association and Association for Educational Communications & Technology. (1998). Information literacy standards for student learning. In *Information power: Building partnerships for learning.* Chicago: Author. Retrieved June 27, 2001, from http://www.ala.org/aasl/ip_nine.html

Anselmi, Dina L., & Law, Anne L. (Eds.). (1997). *Questions of gender: Perspectives and paradoxes.* New York: McGraw Hill.

Arbaugh, J.B. (2000). An exploratory study of the effects of gender on student learning and class participation in an Internet-based MBA course. *Management Learning, 31,* 503-519.

Association of College & Research Libraries. (2000). *Information literacy competency standards for higher education.* Chicago: Author. Retrieved June 27, 2001, from http://www.ala.org/acrl/ilintro.html

Austerlic, Silvia. (1999). Internet, emergent culture and design. In Wendy Harcourt (Ed.), *Women@Internet: Creating new cultures in cyberspace* (pp. 69-75). London: ZedBooks.

Baldwin, George D. (1995). Computer-mediated communication and American Indian education. In Zane L. Berge & Mauri P. Collins (Eds.), *Computer mediated communication and the online classroom: Vol. 1. Overview and perspectives* (pp.113-136). Cresskill, NJ: Hampton Press.

Balka, Ellen. (1996, April). Gender and skill in human computer interaction. Paper delivered at Common Ground, CHI 96, the ACM SIGCHI conference on human factors in computing systems, Vancouver, BC. Retrieved July 2, 2001, from http://www.uni-paderborn .de/StaffWeb/chi96/ElPub/WWW/chi96www/intpost/ Balka/be_txt.html

Bannerji, Himani. (2000). The paradox of diversity: The construction of a multicultural Canada and "women of color." *Women's Studies International Forum, 23(5),* 537-560.

Barber, Simon. (2001, April 18). New initiative will open the wired world to the have-nots. *Business Day (Johannesburg).* Retrieved June 27, 2001, from http:// allafrica.com/stories/printable/200104180094.html

Barrett, E., & Lally, V. (1999, March). Gender differences in an on-line learning environment. *Journal of Computer Assisted Learning, 15,* 48-60.

Baym, Nancy. (1995). The emergence of community in computer mediated communication. In Steve Jones (Ed.), *Cybersociety: Computer-mediated communication and community* (pp. 139-163). Thousand Oaks, CA: Sage.

Bear, John, & Bear, Mariah P. (2001). *Bears' guide to earning college degrees by distance learning.* Berkeley, CA: Ten Speed Press.

Belenky, Mary Field, Clinchy, Blythe McVicker, Goldberger, Nancy Rule, & Tarule, Jill Mattuck. (1986). *Women's ways of knowing: The development of self, voice, and mind.* New York: Basic Books.

Bell, Vicki, & de La Rue, Denise. (n.d.). *Gender harassment on the Internet.* Retrieved June 27, 2001, from http://www.gsu.edu/~lawppw/lawand.papers/harass.html#Herring

Benn, Roseanne, Elliott, Jane, & Whaley, Pat (Eds.). (1998). *Educating Rita and her sisters: Women and continuing education.* Leicester, England: National Institute of Adult Continuing Education.

Berge, Zane L., &. Collins, Mauri P. (1995). *Computer mediated communication and the online classroom: Vol. 1. Overview and perspectives.* Cresskill, NJ: Hampton Press.

Bimber, Bruce. (2000, Fall). Measuring the gender gap on the Internet. *Social Science Quarterly, 81,* 868-876.

Bliss, Joan, Säljö, Roger, & Light, Paul (Eds.). (1999). *Learning sites: Social and technological resources for learning.* Amsterdam: Pergamon.

Blum, Kimberly Dawn. (1998). Gender differences in CMC-based distance education. *Feminista! 2(5).* Retrieved June 27, 2001, from http://www.feminista .com/v2n5/blum.html

Blum, Kimberly Dawn. (1999). Gender differences in asynchronous learning in higher education: Learning styles, participation barriers and communication patterns. *Journal of Asynchronous Learning Environments, 3(1).* Retrieved June 27, 2001, from http://www.aln.org/alnweb/journal/Vol3_issue1/blum.htm

Blumenstyk, Goldie. (2000, December 1). Digital-library company plans to charge students a fee for access.*The Chronicle of Higher Education,* p. A41.

Britain, Sandy, & Liber, Oleg. (n.d.). *A framework for pedagogical evaluation of virtual learning environments.* Retrieved June 27, 2001, from http://www.jtap.ac.uk/reports/htm/jtap-041.html

Brown, John Seely. (2000, March/April). Growing up digital: How the web changes work, education, and the ways people learn. *Change: The Magazine of Higher Learning,* 10-20. Retrieved June 27, 2001, from http://www.aahe.org/change/digital.pdf

Bruckman, Amy S. (1993, August). *Gender swapping on the Internet.* Paper presented at INET '93 in San Francisco, CA. Reston, VA: The Internet Society. Retrieved July 2, 2001, from http://ftp.game.org/pub/mud/text/research/gender-swapping.txt

Burbules, Nicholas C., & Callister, Thomas A., Jr. (2000). *Watch IT: The risks and promises of information technologies for education.* Boulder, CO: Westview Press.

Burge, Elizabeth. (1998). Gender in distance education. In Chère Campbell Gibson (Ed.), *Distance learners in higher education: Institutional responses for quality outcomes* (pp.25-45). Madison, WI: Atwood.

Burge, Elizabeth J. (1999). Using learning technologies: Ideas for keeping one's balance. *Educational Technology, 39(6),* 45-49.

Burge, Elizabeth, & Lenksyj, Helen. (1990). Women studying in distance education: Issues and principles. *CADE: Journal of Distance Education/Revue de l'enseignement à distance, 5,* 1. Retrieved June 27, 2001, from http://cade.athabascau.ca/vol5.1/9_burge_and_lenskyj.html

Burgstahler, Sheryl. (1998, January). Making web pages universally accessible. *CMC Magazine.* Retrieved June 27, 2001, from http://www.december.com/cmc/mag/1998/jan/burg.html

Burke, Catherine. (2000). *Time and space for women: Distance learning and domestic constraints.* Retrieved June 27, 2001, from http://www.com.unisa.edu.au/cccc/papers/refereed/paper6/paper6-1.htm

Campbell, Katy. (1999/2000). The promise of computer-based learning: Designing for inclusivity. In Mary Wyer & Alison Adam (Eds.), Gender and computer technologies [Special issue]. *IEEE Technology and Society Magazine, 18(4),* 28-34.

Card, Karen A., & Horton, Laura. (2000). Providing access to graduate education using computer-mediated communication. *International Journal of Instructional Media, 27(3),* 235-243.

Carmack, Nancy A. (1992). Women and illiteracy: The need for gender specific programming in literacy education. *Adult Basic Education, 2(3),* 176-194.

Carnevale, Dan. (1999, December 2). On-line courses of 1,000 students will become common, industry group says. *The Chronicle of Higher Education*. Retrieved June 27, 2001, from http://chronicle.com/free/99/12/99120201u.htm

Carnevale, Dan. (2001, January 12). It's education online. It's someplace you aren't. What's it called? *The Chronicle of Higher Education,* p. A33.

Carnevale, Dan. (2001, January 19). Education dept. told that aid rules impede distance education. *The Chronicle of Higher Education,* p. A33.

Carr, Sarah. (2001, May 11). Union publishes guide citing high cost of distance education. *The Chronicle of Higher Education,* p. A39.

Castells, Manuel. (1998). *The information age: Economy, society and culture: Vol. 3. End of millennium.* Oxford, England: Blackwell.

Chambers, Mark. (1999). Efficacy and ethics of using digital multimedia. In Alan Tait & Roger Mills (Eds.), *The convergence of distance and conventional education: Patterns of flexibility for the individual learner* (pp. 5-16). London: Routledge.

Chapman, Gerianne. (1998). Factors affecting student attitudes and use of computer-mediated communication in traditional college courses. *Journal of Instruction Delivery Systems, 12*(4), 21-25.

Children's Partnership. (2000). *Online content for low-income and underserved Americans: The digital divide's new frontier—a strategic audit of activities and opportunities.* Retrieved June 27, 2001, from http://www.childrenspartnership.org/pub/low_income/index.html

Coats, Maggie. (1993). *Women's education.* Buckingham, England: Society for Research Into Higher Education and Open University Press.

Cohee, Gail E., Däumer, Elisabeth, Kemp, Theresa D., Krebs, Paula M., Lafky, Sue, & Runzo, Sandra (Eds.). (1998). *The feminist teacher anthology: Pedagogies and classroom strategies.* New York: Teachers College Press.

Collins-Jarvis, Lori. (1997). *Discriminatory messages and gendered power relations in on-line discussion groups.* Paper presented at the 1997 annual meeting of the National Communication Association, Chicago.

Cookson, Peter S. (2000). Implications of Internet technologies for higher education: North American perspectives. *Open Learning, 15*(1), 71-80.

Cooper, Mark N. (2000). *Disconnected, disadvantaged, and disenfranchised: Explorations in the digital divide.* Washington, DC: Consumer Federation of America. Retrieved July 3, 2001, from http://www.consumersunion.org/pdf/disconnect.pdf

Cornwell, Nancy. (1998). Rethinking free expression in the feminist classroom: The problem of hate speech. *Feminist Teacher, 12*(2), 107-118.

Cox, Ana Marie. (2000, December 1). Study sows colleges' dependence on their part-time instructors. *The Chronicle of Higher Education,* pp. A12-14.

Crandall, Robert W. (2000, December). *Universal service, equal access, and the digital divide.* Retrieved June 27, 2001, from http://www.ccst.ucr.edu/cpa/bdd/Crandall.pdf

Damer, Bruce. (1998). *Avatars! Exploring and building virtual worlds on the Internet.* Berkeley, CA: Peachpit Press.

Deaux, Kay. (1997). Commentary: Sorry, wrong number—a reply to gentile's call. In Dina L. Anselmi, & Anne L. Law (Eds.), *Questions of gender: Perspectives and paradoxes* (pp. 21-23). New York: McGraw Hill.

DeFrancisco, Victoria Leto, Fabos, Bettina, & Rodamilans, Tania. (2000). *The disconnections of distance learning: A longitudinal qualitative study.* Unpublished manuscript.

Dewhurst, David G., Macleod, Hamish A., & Norris, Tracey A.M. (2000). Independent student learning aided by computers: An acceptable alternative to lectures? *Computers & Education, 35,* 223-241.

Diamond, Jered. (1997). The Curse of QWERTY. *Discovery, 18*(4), 35-42. Retrieved July 5, 2001, from http://www.discover.com/archive/

Dilger, Bradley. (2000). The ideology of ease. *Journal of Electronic Publishing, 6*(1). Retrieved June 27, 2001, from http://www.press.umich.edu/jep/06-01/dilger.html

The distance learner's guide (1999). Upper Saddle River, NJ: Prentice Hall. Companion website retrieved June 27, 2001, from http://cw.prenhall.com/bookbind/pubbooks/wcet/

Donaldson, Joe F., Graham, Steven W., Martindill, William, & Bradley, Shane. (2000). Adult undergraduate students: How do they define their experiences and their success? *The Journal of Continuing Higher Education, 48*(2), 2-11.

Donath, Judith, Karahalios, Karrie, & Viégas. Fernanda. (1999). Visualizing conversation. *Journal of Computer-Mediated Communication, 4*(1). Retrieved June 27, 2001, from http://www.ascusc.org/jcmc/vol4/issue4/donath.html

Ebben, Maureen. (1994). *Women on the net: An exploratory study of gender dynamics on the soc.women computer network.* Unpublished dissertation, University of Illinois at Urbana-Champaign.

An educator's guide to gender bias issues (n.d.). Retrieved June 27, 2001, from http://lrs.ed.uiuc.edu/wp/access/gender.html

An educator's guide to visual disabilities (n.d.). Retrieved June 27, 2001, from http://lrs.ed.uiuc.edu/wp/access/visual.html

Elmer, Greg. (1999, January). Web rings as computer-mediated communication. *CMC Magazine.* Retrieved June 27, 2001, from http://www.december.com/cmc/mag/1999/jan/elmer.html

Elsdon, Konrad, Reynolds, John, & Stewart, Susan. (1995). *Voluntary organisations: Citizenship, learning and change.* Leicester, England: National Institute of Adult Continuing Education.

Feenberg, Andrew. (1989). The written world: On the theory and practice of computer conferencing. In R. Mason & A. Kaye (Eds.), *Mindweave: Communication, computers and distance education,* pp. 22-39. Oxford, England: Pergamon. Retrieved July 3, 2001, from http://www.rohan.sdsu.edu/faculty/feenberg/Writworl.htm

Fjortoft, Nancy F. (1995, October). *Predicting persistence in distance learning programs.* Paper presented at the Mid-Western Educational Research Meeting, Chicago. (ERIC Document Reproduction Service No. ED387620)

Fordham, Signithia. (1993). "Those loud black girls": (Black) women, silence, and gender "passing" in the academy. *Anthropology and Education Quarterly, 24*(1), 3-32.

Foster, Andrea L. (2000, October 27). Logging in with Melvin I. Urofsky. *The Chronicle of Higher Education,* p. A44.

French, Deanie, Hale, Charles, Johnson, Charles, & Farr, Gerald (Eds.). (1998). *Internet based learning: An introduction and framework for higher education and business.* Sterling, VA: Stylus.

Friedman, Batya, Brok, Eric, Roth, Susan King, & Thomas, John. (1996). Report: Minimizing bias in computer systems. *SIGCHI Bulletin, 28*(1). Retrieved June 27, 2001, from http://www.acm.org/sigchi/bulletin/1996.1/friedman.html

Fürst, Gunilla. (1999). *Sweden—The equal way.* Stockholm: Swedish Institute.

Furst-Bowe, Julie Anne. (2000, September). *Identifying the needs of adult women learners in distance education programs.* Paper presented at the 19th Annual Midwest Research-to-Practice Conference, Madison, WI.

Gay, Geneva. (2000). *Culturally responsive teaching: Theory, research, and practice.* New York: Teachers College Press.

Glaser, Barney G., & Strauss, Anselm L. (1967). *The discovery of grounded theory: Strategies for qualitative research.* New York: Aldine De Gruyter.

Graham, Gordon. (1999). *The Internet: A philosophical inquiry.* London: Routledge.

Green, Susan K., Lightfoot, Mary Ann, Bandy, Carole, & Buchanan, Dale Richard. (1985). A general model of the attribution process. *Basic and Applied Social Psychology, 6,* 159-179.

Gubar, Susan. (2000). *Critical condition: Feminism at the turn of the century.* New York: Columbia University Press.

Guri-Rosenblit, Sarah. (1999). *Distance and campus universities: Tensions and interactions, a comparative study of five countries.* Oxford, England: Pergamon.

Guzzetti, Barbara, & Hynd, Cynthia (Eds.). (1998). *Perspectives on conceptual change: Multiple ways to understand knowing and learning in a complex world.* Mahwah, NJ: Lawrence Erlbaum Associates.

Hammond, Michael. (2000). Communication within on-line forums: The opportunities, the constraints and the value of a communicative approach. *Computers & Education, 35*(4), 251-262.

Haraway, Donna. (1991). *Simians, cyborgs and women: The reinvention of nature.* London: Free Association Books.

Harcourt, Wendy (Ed.). (1999). *Women@Internet: Creating new cultures in cyberspace.* London: ZedBooks.

Harding, Sandra. (1997). Multicultural and global feminist philosophies of science: Resources and challenges. In Lynn Hankinson Nelson & Jack Nelson (Eds.), *Feminism, science and the philosophy of science* (pp. 263-287). Amsterdam: Kluwer Academic.

Harry, Keith, & Perraton, Hilary. (1999). Open and distance learning for the new society. In Keith Harry (Ed.), *Higher education through open and distance learning* (pp. 1-12). London: Routledge.

Hawisher, Gail E. (2000). Accessing the virtual worlds of cyberspace. *Journal of Electronic Publishing, 6*(1). Retrieved June 27, 2001, from http://www.press.umich.edu/jep/06-01/hawisher.html

Hawisher, Gail E. (2000, April). *Inspiring women: Coming to literacy in the information age.* Paper presented at the Conference on College Composition and Communication, Minneapolis, MN.

Hawisher, Gail E., & Moran, Charles. (1997). Responding to writing on-line. In Mary Deane Sorcinelli & Peter Elbow (Eds.), *Writing to learn: Strategies for assigning and responding to writing across the disciplines* (pp.115-125). San Francisco: Jossey-Bass.

Hawisher, Gail E., & Selfe, Cynthia L. (1993). Tradition and change in computer-supported writing environments: A call for action. In Phyllis Kahaney, Linda A.M. Perry, & Joseph Janangelo (Eds.), *Theoretical and critical perspectives on teacher change* (pp.155-186). Norwood, NJ: Ablex.

Hawisher, Gail E., & Selfe, Cynthia L. (1999a). *Global literacies and the World Wide Web.* New York: Routledge.

Hawisher, Gail E., & Selfe, Cynthia L. (1999b). *Passions, pedagogies, and 21st century technologies.* Urbana, IL: National Council of Teachers of English.

Hayles, N. Katherine. (1995). The life cycle of cyborgs: Writing the posthuman. In Chris Hables Gray (with Steven Mentor & Heidi Figueroa-Sarriera) (Eds.), *The cyborg handbook* (pp. 321-335). New York: Routledge.

Headlam, Bruce. (2000, May 25). Boys will be boys, and sometimes girls, in online communities. *New York Times,* Sect. 8, p. 8.

Healy, Patrick. (2000, December 3). Laptops pose new challenge on campus. *The Boston Globe,* p. A1.

Hegarty, Michael, Phelan, Anne, & Kilbride, Lisa. (1998). *Classrooms for distance teaching & learning: A blueprint.* Dublin: Leuven University Press.

Herman, Lee, & Mandell, Alan. (1999). On access: Toward opening the lifeworld toward adult higher education systems. In Alan Tait & Roger Mills (Eds.), *The convergence of distance and conventional education: Patterns of flexibility for the individual learner* (pp.17-38). London: Routledge.

Herring, Susan C. (1998, September 25). *Virtual gender performances.* Talk presented at Texas A&M University, College Station, TX.

Herring, Susan C. (1999). The rhetorical dynamics of gender harassment on-line. In Laura J. Gurak (Ed.), The rhetorics of gender in computer-mediated communication [Special issue]. *The Information Society, 15*(3), 151-167.

Herring, Susan C. (2000, Winter). Gender differences in CMC: Findings and implications. *The CPSR Newsletter, 18*(1). Retrieved June 27, 2001, from http://www.cpsr.org/publications/newsletters/issues/2000/Winter2000/herring.html

Herring, Susan C. (in press). Gender and power in online communication. In Janet Holmes & Miriam Meyerhoff (Eds.), *The handbook of language and gender.* Oxford, England: Blackwell.

Herring, Susan C. (Ed.). (n.d.). *Computer-mediated conversation*. Manuscript submitted for publication.

Herring, Susan C., Johnson, Deborah A., & DiBenedetto, Tamra. (1992). Participation in electronic discourse in a "feminist" field. In Kira Hall, Mary Bucholtz, & Birch Moonwomon (Eds.), *Locating power: Proceedings of the Second Berkeley Women and Language Conference* (pp. 250-262). Berkeley, CA: Berkeley Women & Language Group.

Herring, Susan C., Johnson, Deborah A., & DiBenedetto, Tamra. (1995). "This discussion is going too far!" Male resistance to female participation on the Internet. In Kira Hall & Mary Bucholtz (Eds.), *Gender articulated: Language and the socially constructed self* (pp. 67-96). Berkeley, CA: Berkeley Women & Language Group.

Herring, Susan C., & Nix, Carole. (1997, March). *Is "serious chat" an oxymoron? Academic vs. social uses of Internet relay chat*. Paper presented at the American Association for Applied Linguistics, Orlando, FL.

Hert, Philippe. (1997). Social dynamics of an on-line scholarly debate. *The Information Society, 13,* 329-360.

Hochschild, Arlie Russell. (1989). *The second shift: Working parents and the revolution at home.* New York: Viking Press.

Home, Alice M. (1998). Predicting role conflict, overload and contagion in adult women university students with families and jobs. *Adult Education Quarterly, 48*(2), 85-97.

Huba, Mary E., & Freed, Jann E. (2000). *Learner-centered assessment on college campuses: Shifting the focus from teaching to learning.* Boston: Allyn & Bacon.

Huff, Charles, & Cooper, Joel. (1987). Sex bias in educational software: The effect of designers' stereotypes on the software they design. *Journal of Applied Social Psychology, 17,* 519-532.

Inglehart, Marita, Brown, Donald R., & Vida, Mina. (1994). Competition, achievement, and gender: A stress theoretical analysis. In Paul R. Pintrich, Donald R. Brown, & Claire Ellen Weinstein (Eds.), *Student motivation, cognition, and learning* (pp. 311-329). Hillsdale, NJ: Lawrence Erlbaum Associates.

Ingram, Albert L., Hathorn, Lesley G., & Evans, Alan. (2000). Beyond chat on the Internet. *Computers & Education, 35*(1), 21-35.

International Women's University (IFU). (2000). *Towards the future of the International Women's University.* Hannover, Germany: Author.

Johnson, Scott D., Aragon, Steven R., Shaik, Najmuddin, & Palma-Rivas, Nilda. (2000). Comparative analysis of learner satisfaction and learning outcomes in online and face-to-face learning environments. *Journal of Interactive Learning Research, 11*(1), 29-49.

Johnson-Bailey, Juanita, & Cervero, Ronald M. (1996). An analysis of the educational narratives of reentry women. *Adult Education Quarterly, 45,* 142-157.

Jones, Terry, & Young, Gale Auletta. (1997). Classroom dynamics: Disclosing the hidden curriculum. In Ann Intili Morey & Margie K. Kitano (Eds.), *Multicultural course transformation in higher education: A broader truth* (pp. 89-103). Boston: Allyn & Bacon.

Kimbrough, Doris R. (1999). On-line "chat-room" tutorials—an unusual gender bias in computer use. *Journal of Science Education and Technology, 8*(3), 227-234.

Kirkpatrick, Denise, & Jakupee, Victor. (1999). Becoming flexible: What does it mean? In Alan Tait & Roger Mills (Eds.), *The convergence of distance and conventional education: Patterns of flexibility for the individual learner* (pp. 51-70). London: Routledge.

Kirkup, Gill. (1995, July). *The importance of gender as a category in open and distance learning*. Paper presented at the conference Putting the Student First: Learner Centered Approaches in Open and Distance Learning, Churchill College, Cambridge, England.

Kirkup, Gill. (1998). The potential of the Internet for women's education. In Mechtild Hauff, Gill Kirkup, & Christine von Prümmer (Eds.), *Frauenvorträge an der Fern Universität, 25* (pp. 3-18).

Kirkup, Gill. (1999). A computer of one's own (with an Internet connection!). *Adults Learning, 10*(8), 23-25.

Kirkup, Gill, & von Prümmer, Christine. (1990). Support and connectedness: The needs of women distance education students. *CADE: Journal of Distance Education/Revue de l'enseignement a distance, 5*(2), 9-31.

Kirkup, Gill, & von Prümmer, Christine. (1997). Distance education for European women: The threats and opportunities of new educational forms and media. *The European Journal of Women's Studies, 4*(1), 39-62.

Kitano, Margie K. (1997). A rationale and framework for course change. In Ann Intili Morey & Margie K. Kitano (Eds.), *Multicultural course transformation in higher education: A broader truth* (pp. 1-17). Boston: Allyn & Bacon.

Kliewer, Joy Rosenzweig. (1999). *The innovative campus: Nurturing the distinctive learning environment.* Phoenix, AZ: Oryx Press.

Kolko, Beth E. (2000). Erasing @race: Going white in the (inter)face. In Beth E. Kolko, Lisa Nakamura, & Gilbert B. Rodman (Eds.), *Race in cyberspace* (pp. 213-232). New York: Routledge.

Korenman, Joan, & Wyatt, Nancy. (1996). Group dynamics in an e-mail forum. In Susan Herring (Ed.), *Computer-mediated communication: Linguistic, social and cross-cultural perspectives* (pp. 225-242). Amsterdam: John Benjamins.

Kramarae, Cheris, & Spender, Dale (Eds.). (1994). *The knowledge explosion: Generations of feminist scholarship.* New York: Teachers College Press.

Kramarae, Cheris, & Taylor, H. Jeane. (1993). Women and men on electronic networks. In H. Jeane Taylor, Cheris Kramarae, & Maureen Ebben (Eds.), *Women, information technology and scholarship.* Urbana: University of Illinois Press.

Kramer, Jana, & Kramarae, Cheris. (1997). Gender ethics on the Internet. In Josina M. Makau & Ronald C. Arnett (Eds.), *Communication ethics in an age of diversity* (pp. 226-243). Urbana: University of Illinois Press.

Landow, George. (1991). *Hypertext: The convergence of contemporary critical theory and technology.* Baltimore: John Hopkins University Press.

Law, Cheryl. (1998). Accrediting women, normalising women. In Roseanne Benn, Jane Elliott, & Pat Whaley (Eds.), *Educating Rita and her sisters: Women and continuing education* (pp. 59-64). Leicester, England: National Institute of Adult Continuing Education.

Lee, Raymond M. (2000). *Unobtrusive methods in social research.* Buckingham, England: Open University Press.

Levine, Arthur. (1980). *Why innovation fails.* Albany, NY: State University of New York Press.

Light, V., Nesbitt, E., Light, P., & Burns, J.R. (2000). "Let's you and me have a little discussion": Computer mediated communication in support of campus-based university courses. *Studies in Higher Education, 25,* 85-96.

Littleton, Karen, & Bannert, Maria. (1999). Gender and IT: Contextualising differences. In Joan Bliss, Roger Säljö, & Paul Light (Eds.), *Learning sites: Social and technological resources for learning* (pp. 171-182). Amsterdam: Pergamon.

Livingstone, Sonia. (2000). On the cutting edge, or otherwise, of media and communication research. In Ulla Carlsson (Ed.), 14th Nordic Conference on Media and Communication Research [Special issue]. *Nordicom Review, 21*(2), 7-13.

Livingstone, Sonia, & Bovill, Moira. (1999). *Young people, new media.* London: London School of Economics and Political Science.

Lyall, Robert, & McNamara, Suzanne. (2000). Influences on the orientations to learning of distance education students in Australia. *Open Learning, 15*(2), 107-121.

Magolda, Marcia B. Baxter. (1992). *Knowing and reasoning in college: Gender-related patterns in students' intellectual development.* San Francisco: Jossey-Bass.

Mann, Chris, & Stewart, Fiona. (2000). *Internet communication and qualitative research: A handbook for researching online.* Thousand Oaks, CA: Sage.

Margolis, Jane, Fisher, Allan, & Miller, Faye. (1999/2000). Caring about connections: Gender and computing. In Mary Wyer & Alison Adam (Eds.), Gender and computer technologies [Special issue]. *IEEE Technology and Society Magazine, 18*(4), 13-20. Retrieved June 27, 2001, from http://www.njcc.com/~techsoc/margolis.html

Mason, Robin. (1998). *Globalising education: Trends and applications.* London: Routledge.

Maynard, Elizabeth M., & Pearsall, Simon. J. (1994). What about male mature students? A comparison of the experiences of men and women students. *Journal of Access Studies, 9,* 229-240.

McCarthy, F.T. (2001, February 17). Lessons of a virtual timetable: The promise of online education: The market for e-learning has been slow to take off. What does that say about its future? *The Economist.*

McGivney, Veronica. (1998). Dancing into the future: Developments in adult education. In Roseanne Benn, Jane Elliott, & Pat Whaley (Eds.), *Educating Rita and her sisters: Women and continuing education* (pp. 9-17). Leicester, England: National Institute of Adult Continuing Education.

McKinnon-Slaney, Fiona. (1994). The adult persistence model: A road map to counseling for adult learners. *Journal of Counseling and Development, 72,* 268-275.

Merriam, Sharan B., & Brockett, Ralph G. (1996). *The profession and practice of adult education: An introduction.* San Francisco: Jossey-Bass.

Merullo, Roland. (2000, December 1). Hatred and its sly legacy. *The Chronicle of Higher Education,* pp. B10-B12.

Miller, JoAnn, & Chamberlin, Marilyn. (2000). Women are teachers, men are professors: A study of student perceptions. *Teaching Sociology, 28*(4), 283-298.

Mills, Roger. (1999). Diversity, convergence and the evolution of student support in higher education in the UK. In Alan Tait & Roger Mills (Eds.), *The convergence of distance and conventional education: Patterns of flexibility for the individual learner* (pp. 71-85). London: Routledge.

Mitchell, Timothy. (2000, December). *In the eyes of the beholder: Individual perceptions of technology and education.* Paper and journal entries prepared for Community Development and Network Technology graduate course at Georgetown University.

Mitra, Ananda, Lenzmeier, Stefne, Steffensmeier, Timothy, Avon, Rachel, Qu, Nancy, & Hazen, Mike. (2000). Gender and computer use in an academic institution: Report from a longitudinal study. *Journal of Educational Computing Research, 23*(1), 67-84.

Moran, Joseph J. (1996). *Assessing adult learning: A guide for practitioners.* Malabar, FL: Krieger.

National Education Association. (2000a). *Distance education: Challenges and opportunities.* Retrieved June 27, 2001, from http://www.nea.org/cet/BRIEFS/brief7.html

National Education Association. (2000b). *Technology and gender inequity.* Retrieved June 27, 2001, from http://www.nea.org/cet/BRIEFS/brief5.html

National Election Study. (1998). *American national election study, 1998 pre- and post-election survey.* Ann Arbor, MI: The University of Michigan Institute for Social Research Center for Political Studies.

Nelson, Harold, & Stolterman, Erik. (2000, July). Design as being in service. In David Durling & Ken Friedman (Eds.), *Proceedings of the conference Doctoral Education in Design: Foundations for the Future* (pp. 23-33). Staffordshire, England: Staffordshire University Press.

Noll, Roger G., Older-Aguilar, Dina, Rosston, Gregory L., & Ross, Richard R. (2000, December). The digital divide: Definitions, measurement, and policy issues. In *Bridging the Digital Divide,* California Public Affairs Forum held at Stanford University, Stanford, CA. Retrieved June 27, 2001, from http://www.ccst.ucr.edu/cpa/bdd/bddhome.html

Palloff, Rena M., & Pratt, Keith. (1999). *Building learning communities in cyberspace: Effective strategies for the online classroom.* San Francisco: Jossey-Bass.

Parry, Shirley C. (1996). Feminist pedagogy and techniques for the changing classroom. In Curriculum transformation in community colleges: Focus on introductory courses [Special edition]. *Women's Studies Quarterly, 3*(4), 45-54.

Passerini, Katia, & Granger, Mary J. (2000). A developmental model for distance learning using the Internet. *Computers & Education, 34,* 1-15.

Passig, David, & Levin, Haya. (1999). Gender interest differences with multimedia learning interfaces. *Computers in Human Behavior, 15*(2) 173-183.

Pear, Robert. (2000, November 5). Far more single mothers are taking jobs. *New York Times,* Sect. 1, p. 28.

Pearson, Carol S., Shavlik, Donna L., & Touchton, Judith G. (Eds.). (1989). *Educating the majority: Women challenge tradition in higher education.* New York: Macmillan.

Pew Internet & American Life Project. (2000, May). *Tracking online life: How women use the Internet to cultivate relationships with family and friends.* Retrieved July 2, 2001, from http://www.pewinternet.org/reports/toc.asp?Report=11

Pew Internet & American Life Project. (2001, February 18). *More online, doing more: 16 million newcomers gain Internet access in the last half of 2000 as women, minorities, and families with modest incomes continue to surge online.* Retrieved June 27, 2001, from http://www.pewinternet.org/reports/toc.asp?Report=30

Powell, Rick, McGuire, Sharon, & Crawford, Gail. (1999). Convergence of student types: Issues for distance education. In Alan Tait & Roger Mills (Eds.), *The convergence of distance and conventional education: Patterns of flexibility for the individual learner* (pp. 86-99). London: Routledge.

Questions facing academe in the electronic era. (2000, November 10). *Chronicle of Higher Education,* p. B21.

Reeves, Byron, & Nass, Clifford. (1996). *The media equation: How people treat computers, television, and new media like real people and places.* Stanford, CA: CSLI Publications.

Reid, Elizabeth M. (1994). *Cultural formations in text-based virtual realities.* Unpublished master's thesis, University of Melbourne, Melbourne, Australia.

Rendon, Jim. (2000, September 12). Learning potential. *The Industry Standard.* Retrieved June 28, 2001, from http://www.thestandard.com/article/display/0,1151,18232,00.html

Richardson, Helen J., & French, Sheila. (2000). Education on-line: What's in it for women? In Ellen Balka & Richard Smith (Eds.), *Women, work and computerization: Charting a course to the future* (pp. 300-307). Boston: Kluwer Academic.

Richardson, Julie Ann, & Turner, Anthony. (2000). A large-scale "local" evaluation of students' learning experiences using virtual learning environments. In Martin Oliver (Ed.), Evaluation of learning technology [Special issue]. *Educational Technology & Society, 3*(4), 1-16.

Roberts, Lynne D., & Parks, Malcolm R. (1999). The social geography of gender switching in virtual environments on the Internet. *Information, Communication, & Society, 2*(4), 521-540.

Rodino, M. (1997). Breaking out of binaries: Reconceptualizing gender and its relationship to language in computer-mediated communication. *Journal of Computer Mediated-Communication, 3*(3). Retrieved June 28, 2001, from http://www.ascusc.org/jcmc/vol3/issue3/rodino.html

Ross-Gordon, Jovita, & Brown-Haywood, Felicia. (2000). Keys to college success as seen through the eyes of African American adult students. *The Journal of Continuing Higher Education, 48*(3), 14-23.

Ruark, Jennifer. (2000, November 10). Cultural influences on how the brain works: Interview with Robert E. Nisbett. *The Chronicle of Higher Education,* p. A16.

Sanchez, Claudio. (2000, August). Changing face of America. *Morning Edition.* National Public Radio.

Sandler, Bernice Resnick, Silverberg, Lisa A., & Hall, Roberta M. (1996). *The chilly classroom climate: A guide to improve the education of women.* Washington, DC: National Association of Women in Education.

Sayers, Tamara. (1999). Internet technology: Merely a tool? *Women'space, 4*(1), 20, 22.

Scheibe, Karl E. (2000). *The drama of everyday life.* Cambridge, MA: Harvard University Press.

Schwab, Peter, & Pollis, Adamantia. (2000). Globalization's impact on human rights. In Adamantia Pollis & Peter Schwab (Eds.), *Human rights: New perspectives, new realities* (pp. 209-223). London: Lynne Rienner.

Sconce, Jeffrey. (2000). *Haunted media: Electronic presence from telegraphy to television.* Durham, NC: Duke University Press.

Selfe, Cynthia L. (2000). *Studying the acquisition and development of technological literacy.* Manuscript in preparation.

Selfe, Cynthia L. (2000, April). *Technological literacy in America: Collecting the stories.* Paper presented at the Conference on College Composition and Communication, Minneapolis, MN.

Selfe, Cynthia L., & Selfe, Richard J., Jr. (1994). The politics of the interface: Power and its exercise in electronic contact zones. *College Composition and Communication, 45*(4), 480-504.

Selwyn, Neil. (2000). Research computers and education—glimpses of the wider picture. *Computers & Education 34,* 93-101.

Sherron, Gene T., & Boettcher, Judith V. (1997). *Distance learning: The shift to interactivity: CAUSE Professional Paper Series #17.* Boulder, CO: CAUSE. Retrieved June 28, 2001, from http://www.educause.edu/ir/library/pdf/PUB3017.pdf

Smith, Christine B., McLaughlin, Margaret L., & Osborne, Kerry K. (1997). Conduct controls on Usenet. *Journal of Computer-Mediated Communication, 2*(4). Retrieved June 28, 2001, from http://www.ascusc.org/jcmc/vol2/issue4/smith.html

Sparks, Barbara. (1998). The politics of culture and the struggle to get an education. *Adult Education Quarterly, 48*(4), 245-259.

Spender, Dale. (1995). *Nattering on the Net: Women, power and cyberspace.* Melbourne, Australia: Spinifex.

Spring, Joel. (1995). *The intersection of cultures: Multicultural education in the United States.* New York: McGraw-Hill.

Sproull, Lee, & Kiesler, Sara. (1991). *Connections: New ways of working in the networked organization.* Boston: Massachusetts Institute of Technology.

Stafford, Beth. (2000). Libraries. In Cheris Kramarae & Dale Spender (Eds.), *Routledge international encyclopedia of women: Global women's issues and knowledge, Vol. 3* (pp. 1234-1238). New York: Routledge.

Stalker, J. (1997, July). Women's participation in tertiary education: Misogynistic responses. In *Crossing borders, breaking boundaries: Research in the education of adults.* Proceedings of International Standing Conference on University Teaching and Research in the Education of Adults (SCUTREA), 27th Annual Conference, University of London, England.

Steele, Claude M. (1997). A threat in the air: How stereotypes shape the intellectual identities and performance of women and African Americans. *American Psychologist, 52,* 613-629.

Steele, Claude M., & Aronson, J. (1995). Stereotype threat and the intellectual test performance of African Americans. *Journal of Personality and Social Psychology, 69,* 797-811.

Sutton, Laurel A. (1996). Cocktails and thumbtacks in the Old West: What would Emily Post say. In Lynn Cherny & Elizabeth Reba Weise (Eds.), *Wired women: Gender and new realities in cyberspace* (pp. 169-187). Seattle, WA: Seal Press.

Szabo, Attila, & Hastings, Nigel. (2000). Using IT in the undergraduate classroom: Should we replace the blackboard with PowerPoint? *Computers & Education, 35,* 175-187.

Szabo, Michael. (1995). Enhancing the interactive classroom through computer-based instruction: Some examples from Plato. In Zane L. Berge & Mauri P. Collins (Eds.), *Computer mediated communication and the online classroom: Vol. 1. Overview and perspectives* (pp. 165-169). Cresskill, NJ: Hampton Press.

Tait, Alan, & Mills, Roger. (1999). *The convergence of distance and conventional education: Patterns of flexibility for the individual learner.* London: Routledge.

Taub, Diane E., & Fanflik, Patricia L. (2000, January). The inclusion of disability in introductory sociology textbooks. *Teaching Sociology, 28,* 12-23.

Taylor, H. Jeane, Kramarae, Cheris, & Ebben, Maureen. (1993). *Women, information technology, and scholarship.* Urbana: University of Illinois Press.

Technology as "big magic" and other myths: T&S interview with Langdon Winner. (1998). *IEEE Technology and Society Magazine, 17*(3), 4-16.

Thompson, Jane. (1997). *Words in edgeways: Radical learning for social change.* Leicester, England: National Institute of Adult Continuing Education.

Tisdell, Elizabeth J. (1995). *Creating inclusive adult learning environments: Insights from multicultural education and feminist pedagogy.* (ERIC Document Reproduction Service No. ED384827)

Tisdell, Elizabeth J. (1998). Poststructural feminist pedagogies: The possibilities and limitations of feminist emancipatory adult learning theory and practice. *Adult Education Quarterly, 48*(3), 139-156.

Törpel, Bettina. (2000). Do computers transform people into women and men? In Ellen Balka & Richard Smith (Eds.), *Women, work and computerization: Charting a course to the future* (pp. 17-25). Boston: Kluwer Academic.

Turkle, Sherry. (1988). Computer reticence: Why women fear the intimate machine. In Cheris Kramarae (Ed.), *Technology and women's voices: Keeping in touch* (pp. 41-61). New York: Pergamon.

Turkle, Sherry. (1995). *Life on the screen: Identity in the age of the Internet.* New York: Simon & Schuster.

Turkle, Sherry. (1997). Multiple subjectivity and virtual community at the end of the Freudian century. *Sociological Inquiry, 67,* 72-84.

Turner, Caroline Sotello Viernes, & Myers, Samuel L., Jr. (1999). *Faculty of color in academe: Bittersweet success.* Boston: Allyn & Bacon.

Turoff, Murray. (1999). Education, commerce, and communications: The era of competition. *WebNet Journal, 1*(1), 22-31.

UCLA Center for Communication Policy. (2000). *UCLA Internet report: "Surveying the digital future."* Retrieved July 2, 2001, from http://www.ccp.ucla.edu

UCLA Higher Education Research Institute. (2001). *An overview of the 2000 freshman norms.* Retrieved July 2, 2001, from http://www.gseis.ucla.edu/heri/00_exec_summary.htm

Ullman, Ellen. (1995). Out of time: Reflections on the programming life. In James Brook & Iain A. Boal (Eds.), *Resisting the virtual life: The culture and politics of information* (pp. 131-143). San Francisco: City Lights.

UNESCO Institute for Education. (1997). *Universities and the future of adult learning: Booklet 2a. Universities and adult learning.* Hamburg, Germany: Author. Retrieved July 2, 2001, from http://www.unesco.org/education/uie/confintea/pdf/2a.pdf

Unger, Rhoda K. & Crawford, Mary. (1997). Commentary: Sex and gender—the troubled relationship between terms and concepts. In Dina L. Anselmi & Anne L. Law (Eds.), *Questions of gender: Perspectives and paradoxes* (pp. 18-21). New York: McGraw Hill.

U.S. Bureau of the Census. (1999). *Educational attainment in the United States: March 1998 (update).* Washington, DC: Author. Retrieved July 2, 2001, from http://www.census.gov

U.S. Department of Commerce. (2000). *Falling through the net: Toward digital inclusion: A report on Americans' access to technology tools.* Washington, DC: Author. Retrieved July 2, 2001, from http://www.esa.doc.gov/fttn00.pdf

U.S. Department of Education, National Center for Education Statistics. (1997). *Digest of Education Statistics 1997.* Washington, DC: Author. Retrieved July 2, 2001, from http://nces.ed.gov/pubs/digest97/d970003.html#enrollment

U.S. Department of Education, National Center for Education Statistics. (1999). *Distance education at postsecondary education institutions: 1997-98.* Washington, DC: Author. Retrieved July 2, 2001, from http://nces.ed.gov/pubs2000/2000013.pdf

U.S. Department of Education, Web-Based Education Commission. (2000). *The power of the internet for learning: Moving from promise to practice.* Washington, DC: Author. Retrieved July 2, 2001, from http://www.webcommission.org

U.S. Senate. (2001, March 7). Section-by-section analysis of the "Technology, Education and Copyright Harmonization Act of 2001" or the TEACH Act, H.R. 487, 107th Cong. *Congressional Record, 147,* S2009.

van Oost, Ellen. (2000). Making the computer masculine: The historical roots of gendered representations. In Ellen Balka & Richard Smith (Eds.), *Women, work and computerization: Charting a course to the future* (pp. 9-16). Boston: Kluwer Academic.

Von Holzen, Roger. (2000). A look at the future of higher education. *Syllabus, 14*(4), 56-57, 65.

von Prümmer, Christine. (1993, June). *Women-friendly perspectives in distance education.* Keynote address presented at the International WIN Working Conference, Umeå, Sweden.

Walstrom, Mary, K. (2000). "You know, who's the thinnest?": Combating surveillance and creating safety in coping with eating disorders online. In Janet Morahan-Martin (Ed.), Women and the Internet [Special edition]. *CyberPsychology & Behavior, 3*(5), 761-783.

Warschauer, Mark. (2000). Language, identity, and the Internet. In Beth E. Kolko, Lisa Nakamura, & Gilbert B. Rodman (Eds.), *Race in cyberspace* (pp. 151-170). New York: Routledge.

Weigel, Van. (2000). E-learning and the tradeoff between richness and reach in higher education. *Change: The Magazine of Higher Learning, 33*(5), 33.

White, Candace, & Kinnick, Katherine N. (2000). One click forward and two clicks back: Portrayal of women using computers in television commercials. *Women's Studies in Communication, 23*(3), 392-412.

White, Ken W., & Weight, Bob H. (2000). *The online teaching guide: A handbook of attitudes, strategies, and techniques for the virtual classroom.* Boston: Allyn & Bacon.

Williams, Joan. (2000, December 15). What stymies women's academic careers? It's personal. *The Chronicle of Higher Education,* p. B10.

Wolfe, Joanna. (2000). Gender, ethnicity and classroom discourse: Communication patterns of Hispanic and white students in networked classrooms. *Written Communication, 17,* 491-519.

Wolff, Paula. (2001, March 16). Very part-time students are hobbled by very little financial aid. *The Chronicle of Higher Education,* p. B20.

Wood, Julia T. (1998). *Gendered lives: Communication, gender, and culture* (3rd ed.). Belmont, CA: Wadsworth.

Woodward, Alison, & Lyon, Dawn. (2000). Gendered time and women's access to power. In Mino Vianello & Gwen Moore (Eds.), *Gendering elites: Economic and political leadership in 27 industrialised societies* (pp. 91-103). London: Macmillan.

World Wide Web Consortium. (1999). *Web content accessibility guidelines 1.0: W3C recommendation.* Retrieved July 2, 2001, from http://www.w3.org/TR/1999/WAI-WEBCONTENT-19990505/

Young, Jeffrey. (2000, November 10). MOO's, the old chat rooms, are updated for distance education. *The Chronicle of Higher Education,* p. A47.

AAUW
Equity
Library

AAUW Equity Library

The Third Shift: Women Learning Online

Through distance education, technology offers new opportunities for many women to achieve educational goals. This report explores why women pursue education; how they balance work, family, and education; and what would make distance learning easier for them, and makes recommendations for improvements. 80 pages/2001.
$11.95 AAUW members/$12.95 nonmembers.

Hostile Hallways: Bullying, Teasing, and Sexual Harassment in School

One student in five fears being hurt or bothered in school; four students in five personally experience sexual harassment. These are among the findings of this nationally representative survey of 2,064 eighth- through 11th-graders. The report investigates sexual harassment in public schools, comparing the findings with AAUW's original survey in 1993 and exploring differences in responses by gender, race/ethnicity, grade level, and area (urban or suburban/rural). Conducted by Harris Interactive. 56 pages/2001.
$8.95 AAUW members/$9.95 nonmembers.

Beyond the "Gender Wars": A Conversation About Girls, Boys, and Education

Report of the key insights presented during a symposium convened by the AAUW Educational Foundation in September 2000 to foster a discussion among scholars who study both girls' and boys' experiences in and out of school. Participants share their insights about gender identity and difference, challenge popular views of girls' and boys' behavior, and explore the meaning of equitable education for the 21st century. 60 pages/2001.
$8.95 AAUW members/$9.95 nonmembers.

¡Sí, Se Puede! Yes, We Can: Latinas in School
by Angela Ginorio and Michelle Huston

Comprehensive look at the status of Latina girls in the U.S. public education system. Report explores conflicts between institutional expectations and the realities of student lives and discusses the social, cultural, and community factors that affect Hispanic education. Available in English and Spanish. 84 pages/2001.
$11.95 AAUW members/$12.95 nonmembers.

A License for Bias: Sex Discrimination, Schools, and Title IX

Examines uneven efforts to implement the 1972 civil rights law that protects some 70 million students and employees from sex discrimination in schools and universities. The analysis of non-sports-related complaints filed between 1993 and 1997 pinpoints problems that hamper enforcement and includes recommendations for Congress, the Office for Civil Rights, and educational institutions. 84 pages/2000.
Published by the AAUW Legal Advocacy Fund.
$11.95 AAUW members/$12.95 nonmembers.

Community Coalitions Manual With Lessons Learned From the Girls Can! Project

A comprehensive guide for establishing and sustaining effective coalition-based programs. Covers volunteer recruitment, project planning, evaluation, fundraising, and public relations, with contact information for more than 200 organizations, and lessons learned from the Girls Can! Community Coalitions Projects, a nationwide gender equity program. 172 pages/2000.
$14.95 AAUW members/$16.95 nonmembers.

Tech-Savvy: Educating Girls in the New Computer Age

Explores girls' and teachers' perspectives of today's computer culture and technology use at school, home, and the workplace. Presents recommendations for broadening access to computers for girls and others who don't fit the "male hacker/computer geek" stereotype. 84 pages/2000.
$11.95 AAUW members/$12.95 nonmembers.

Voices of a Generation: Teenage Girls on Sex, School, and Self

Compares the comments of roughly 2,100 girls nationwide on peer pressure, sexuality, the media, and school. The girls participated in AAUW teen forums called Sister-to-Sister Summits. The report explores differences in responses by race, ethnicity, and age and offers action proposals to solve common problems. 95 pages/1999.
$13.95 AAUW members/$14.95 nonmembers.

Gaining a Foothold: Women's Transitions Through Work and College
Examines how and why women make changes in their lives through education. The report profiles three groups—women going from high school to college, from high school to work, and from work back to formal education—using both quantitative and qualitative methods. Report findings include an analysis of women's educational decisions, aspirations, and barriers. 100 pages/1999.
$11.95 AAUW members/$12.95 nonmembers.

Gender Gaps: Where Schools Still Fail Our Children
Measures schools' mixed progress toward gender equity and excellence since the 1992 publication of *How Schools Shortchange Girls: The AAUW Report*. Research compares student course enrollments, tests, grades, risks, and resiliency by race and class as well as gender. It finds some gains in girls' achievement, some areas where boys —not girls—lag, and some areas, like technology, where needs have not yet been addressed. 150 pages/1998.
$12.95 AAUW members/$13.95 nonmembers.

Gender Gaps Executive Summary
Overview of *Gender Gaps* report with selected findings, tables, bibliography, and recommendations for educators and policy-makers. 24 pages/1998.
$6.95 AAUW members/$7.95 nonmembers.

Separated by Sex: A Critical Look at Single-Sex Education for Girls
The foremost educational scholars on single-sex education in grades K-12 compare findings on whether girls learn better apart from boys. The report, including a literature review and a summary of a forum convened by the AAUW Educational Foundation, challenges the popular idea that single-sex education is better for girls than coeducation. 102 pages/1998.
$11.95 AAUW members/$12.95 nonmembers.

Gender and Race on the Campus and in the School: Beyond Affirmative Action Symposium Proceedings
A compilation of papers presented at AAUW's 1997 college/university symposium. Topics include K-12 curricula and student achievement, positive gender and race awareness in elementary and secondary school, campus climate and multiculturalism, higher education student retention and success, and the nexus of race and gender in higher education curricula and classrooms. 428 pages/1997.
$19.95 AAUW members/$21.95 nonmembers.

Girls in the Middle: Working to Succeed in School
Engaging study of middle school girls and the strategies they use to meet the challenges of adolescence. Report links girls' success to school reforms like team teaching and cooperative learning, especially where these are used to address gender issues. 116 pages/1996.
$12.95 AAUW members/$14.95 nonmembers.

Growing Smart: What's Working for Girls in School Executive Summary and Action Guide
Illustrated summary of academic report identifying themes and approaches that promote girls' achievement and healthy development. Based on review of more than 500 studies and reports. Includes action strategies, program resource list, and firsthand accounts of some program participants. 48 pages/1995.
$10.95 AAUW members/$12.95 nonmembers.

How Schools Shortchange Girls: The AAUW Report
A startling examination of how K-12 girls are disadvantaged in America's public schools. Includes recommendations for educators and policy-makers as well as concrete strategies for change. 224 pages/ Marlowe, 1995.
$11.95 AAUW members/$12.95 nonmembers.

SchoolGirls: Young Women, Self-Esteem, and the Confidence Gap
Riveting book by journalist Peggy Orenstein in association with AAUW shows how girls in two racially and economically diverse California communities suffer the painful plunge in self-esteem documented in *Shortchanging Girls, Shortchanging America*. 384 pages/ Doubleday, 1994.
$11.95 AAUW members/$12.95 nonmembers.

Shortchanging Girls, Shortchanging America: Executive Summary
Summary of the 1991 poll that assesses self-esteem, educational experiences, and career aspirations of girls and boys ages 9 through 15. Revised edition reviews poll's impact, offers action strategies, and highlights survey results with charts and graphs. 20 pages/1994.
$8.95 AAUW members/$11.95 nonmembers.

Hostile Hallways: The AAUW Survey on Sexual Harassment in America's Schools
The first national study of sexual harassment in public school, based on the experiences of 1,632 students in grades eight through 11. Report includes gender and ethnic/racial data breakdowns. Conducted by Louis Harris and Associates. 28 pages/1993.
$8.95 AAUW members/$11.95 nonmembers.

ORDER FORM

Name_____ AAUW membership # (if applicable)_____

Street_____

City/State/ZIP _____

Daytime phone (_____)_____ E-mail _____

Item	Price Member/Nonmember	Quantity	Total
The Third Shift: Women Learning Online	$11.95/$12.95	_____	_____
Hostile Hallways: Bullying, Teasing, and Sexual Harassment in School	$ 8.95/$ 9.95	_____	_____
Beyond the "Gender Wars": A Conversation About Girls, Boys, and Education	$ 8.95/$ 9.95	_____	_____
¡Sí, Se Puede! Yes, We Can: Latinas in School (Check one: ❑ English or ❑ Spanish)	$11.95/$12.95	_____	_____
A License for Bias: Sex Discrimination, Schools, and Title IX	$11.95/$12.95	_____	_____
Community Coalitions Manual	$14.95/$16.95	_____	_____
Tech-Savvy: Educating Girls in the New Computer Age	$11.95/$12.95	_____	_____
Voices of a Generation: Teenage Girls on Sex, School, and Self	$13.95/$14.95	_____	_____
Gaining a Foothold: Women's Transitions Through Work and College	$11.95/$12.95	_____	_____
Gender Gaps: Where Schools Still Fail Our Children	$12.95/$13.95	_____	_____
Gender Gaps Executive Summary	$ 6.95/$ 7.95	_____	_____
Separated by Sex: A Critical Look at Single-Sex Education for Girls	$11.95/$12.95	_____	_____
Gender and Race on the Campus and in the School	$19.95/$21.95	_____	_____
Girls in the Middle: Working to Succeed in School	$12.95/$14.95	_____	_____
Growing Smart Executive Summary and Action Guide	$10.95/$12.95	_____	_____
How Schools Shortchange Girls: The AAUW Report	$11.95/$12.95	_____	_____
SchoolGirls: Young Women, Self-Esteem, and the Confidence Gap	$11.95/$12.95	_____	_____
Shortchanging Girls, Shortchanging America—Executive Summary	$ 8.95/$11.95	_____	_____
Hostile Hallways: The AAUW Survey on Sexual Harassment in America's Schools	$ 8.95/$11.95	_____	_____

Subtotal ($25 minimum): _____

Your State Sales Tax: _____

Shipping/Handling (see chart below): _____

Total: _____

For bulk pricing on orders of 10 or more, call 800/225-9998 ext. 537.

For rush orders, call 800/225-9998 ext. 537. A $5 fee plus actual shipping charges will apply.

Shipments to foreign countries are sent surface rate and postage is charged at cost plus a $15 handling charge.

All applicable duties and taxes are paid by customer.

AAUW Federal Identification Number: 53-0025390.

❑ Check/Money Order
   (Please make payable in U.S. currency to Newton Manufacturing Co. Do not send cash.)

❑ MasterCard   ❑ VISA

Shipping and Handling (based on order size)
$25-$49.99 . . . .$7.95
$50-$99.99 . . . .$8.95
$100-$249.99 . .$10.95
$250-$350 . . . .$15.95
Over $350 . . . . .$4.95 plus 5% of subtotal

Card #__ __ __ __ - __ __ __ __ - __ __ __ __ - __ __ __ __   Name on Card _____

Cardholder signature_____ Expiration Date _____

SATISFACTION GUARANTEED: If you are not completely satisfied with your purchase, please return it within 90 days for exchange, credit, or refund. Videos are returnable only if defective and for replacement only.

FOR MAIL ORDERS, SEND THIS FORM TO
   AAUW Sales Office
   Newton Manufacturing Co.
   P.O. Box 927
   Newton, IA 50208-0927

FOR TELEPHONE ORDERS,
   CALL 800/225-9998 ext. 537
   FAX 800/500-5118

FOR ONLINE ORDERS, GO TO www.aauw.org

AAUW
Educational Foundation

The AAUW Educational Foundation provides funds to advance education, research, and self-development for women and to foster equity and positive societal change.

In principle and in practice, the AAUW Educational Foundation values and supports diversity. There shall be no barriers to full participation in this organization on the basis of gender, race, creed, age, sexual orientation, national origin, disability, or class.